SH*T YOU DON'T LEARN IN COLLEGE

MAKE MORE MONEY, HAVE A BIGGER IMPACT, AND BUILD A LIFE WITH MEANING

ZANDER FRYER

PRAISE FOR SH*T YOU DON'T LEARN IN COLLEGE

"Sh*t You Don't Learn In College is a well written account from someone who has lived the journey. If you are stuck in a 9-5 job and you want to know the exact steps you need to take to build a life with more money, more meaning, and more freedom, this is the book to read"

JACK CANFIELD, N.Y. TIMES #1 BESTSELLER, CHICKEN SOUP FOR THE SOUL

"Zander Fryer is an extraordinary entrepreneur. His new book "Sh*t You Don't Learn in College" will help you ride the ups and downs into greater success than you thought possible!"

DR. DEBORAH SANDELLA PHD, RN, #1 INTERNATIONAL BESTSELLER & CREATOR OF THE RIM® METHOD

"A must read for anyone (young or old) looking for more in their life than what 'common knowledge' tells us is possible."

JOSHUA KING, FOUNDER, MANSCAPED

"This book will change your life. It will force you to look at things from an entirely different perspective and give you the tools to take action along the way. There exists a ton of coaching fluff out there today. Zander brings real life, proven, legitimate direction and answers from his and other's success."

JOHN CARNEY, 22-YR CAREER IN THE NFL AND #5 ON THE NFL'S ALL TIME SCORING LIST.

"Zander has finally done it. A clear account as to why college doesn't work for so many of us and what to do instead."

PATTY AUBERY, N.Y. TIMES BEST SELLING AUTHOR

"Zander is the next Tony Robbins. He's kind, caring, courageous and brilliant when it comes to coaching people through business and life. His energy, empathy, and experience - both in his highs and lows - make him the #1 coach I trust... and you should too."

CRAIG BALLANTYNE, BEST SELLING AUTHOR, THE PERFECT DAY FORMULA

"This book will change and transform you. It will force you to look at things from an entirely different perspective and give you the tools to break from an ordinary job and leapfrog into your purpose driven passion."

BEDROS KEUILIAN, FOUNDER OF FIT BODY
BOOT CAMP FRANCHISE AND AUTHOR OF
MAN UP

*For AJ: I'm grateful for all you have taught me,
both in life and death.*

CONTENTS

INTRO

"Advertising has us chasing cars and clothes, working jobs we hate so we can buy shit we don't need... This is your life, and it's ending one minute at a time."

CHUCK PALAHNIUK, *FIGHT CLUB*

Five years ago, I was stuck in a nine-to-five, single, lonely, bored and lost. I was unfulfilled, unhappy, and getting paid a quarter million dollars a year at tech giant Cisco Systems to stay that way. To nearly everybody else, it looked like I had hit the jackpot. I was living the life in California: partying every weekend, going on fun vacations and buying all kinds of cool stuff... but I felt empty. And after losing my best friend to suicide when I was 28, I realized that everything I was doing was a desperate attempt to feel something — anything. I was craving fulfilment and connection, and even though I was more comfortable than most people would ever be, I knew I needed to get out.

Now, as I'm working on this book, I'm sitting in a beautiful house on a clifftop in Sedona. It's 7 a.m. and I'm looking out over one of the most incredible landscapes I've ever seen. A hawk just flew by, and the sun is starting to light up the mountain in front of me. My amazing wife Maddy, the love of my life, is asleep in the bedroom, enjoying some well-earned time off from the multi-million dollar company we run together. We live on the beach in San Diego and travel to amazing new places around the world, and we came up here for a week to recharge — to meditate, write, and hang out together, while our team continues to grow the business and make money.

Since quitting my job at Cisco five years ago, I've...

- Made over $8 million in my business
- Been featured on the Inc. 5000 list
- Married a sexy Australian goddess
- Networked with (and been hired by) professional athletes, award winning musicians, Hollywood actors, and billionaires
- Spoken on stage in front of thousands (including a TEDx Talk)
- Travelled to dozens of exotic locations for work and play like Costa Rica, Tulum, Australia, Greece, and Albuquerque (okay, maybe not *all* the best places)
- Planted over 5,000 trees to restore the rainforests and supported over 10,000 families struggling just to get clean water every day

I don't say all this to brag. I say this to show you what's possible in a very short period of time when you commit to making it happen.

Because if you'd told me five years ago that this would be my life, I would have laughed in your face. It's literally a dream life. I couldn't ask for anything more. And a version of this life is possible for you too — you just don't have the knowledge yet to make your dreams become reality. I truly believe that when we couple the right knowledge, with a strong desire for action, anything is possible. The problem is, most of us are never given the right knowledge — the Sh*t You Don't Learn In College.

Before we go any further, though, I want you to imagine yourself in five years. Imagine waking up on yet another Monday morning, staring at the ceiling while your alarm blares beside you. Feel the tightness in your chest, the stress that pulses through your body as you think about walking into your office, dealing with all the bullshit again, knowing that you're going to be doing this for *the rest of your life*. Yeah, you might live in a bigger house. You might have a nicer car, some fancier clothes, a bigger bank account. You might even have a different partner. But it's still the same unfulfilled life. Same bullshit day in and day out. All the same frustrations and limits and fears — just five years more entrenched in your body and mind as your lot in life.

I don't want that to happen to you. I've seen so many people get stuck exactly where they are because they're too afraid to take a risk and try something *different*. Bestselling author and coach Mel Robbins puts it like this: "If you don't start doing the things you don't feel like doing, you will wake up one year from today and be in exactly the same place."

That sucks, but it doesn't have to be that way. Look, I get it — it's not that easy to just snap your fingers and start doing things differently. Traditional career advice is not working anymore. Traditional financial advice is not working anymore. Traditional family lives and spiritual practices and social roles are now in flux. The things that worked for our parents and grandparents don't work for us, and that means we have to take the reins and actively figure out what matters. We have to figure out what we care about, and then work out how to build a life and a career specifically around those priorities.

This book is for you whether you want to be an entrepreneur or an 'intrapreneur' inside someone else's business. It will work whether you're in a 9-to-5 right now and are dreaming of starting your own thing, or if you want to build an entrepreneurial mindset so that you can find a role you can own inside a more meaningful business. Either way when you implement these tools you will be more aligned with your work, build a career you love, make more money and have more freedom than you ever thought possible. I believe that everybody has some form of entrepreneurship in them. Before the Industrial Revolution and the growth of the corporation, most people were self-employed or had a specific role within their community. You developed a profession or an area of expertise, and carved out a niche for yourself. Entrepreneurship is creative, and creativity is human. It's in our blood — you have all the right stuff already — but your ability to be an entrepreneur stems from your ability to be true to yourself. You have to be aligned with your true self to become an entrepreneur, and this book is designed to help you do that.

All that this requires from you is what I call the "entrepreneurial mindset", and the willingness to do the work. You don't have to be an actual entrepreneur yet — you could be 18 years old or you could be 55; you could be a million-dollar business owner or work full-time as an administrative assistant — but you do have to have the attitude that change is possible, and that with the right tools and the right guidance, you can absolutely have the life you want, with more money, a bigger impact, and more meaning.

You know the old way doesn't work. You know that there is a crazy amount of opportunity out there for people who can spot it. And you know you have so much more to give. So if that's you, you're in the right place. You can do this. My promise to you is that I will give it to you straight. I am not going to sugar coat anything in this book. I'm a blunt kind of guy, and I'm not going to coddle you because it's not going to help you. Working with the coaches in my business, High Impact Coaching, we call this the 'soft front, firm back' approach. I have all the love in the world for our coaches and all our students — including you — and I have got your back 100% of the way. But I'm also going to tell you when you're falling short or when you need to get your ass into gear. If you can work with that, you're already on your way.

My goal is that this book will help you make more money, have a bigger impact, *and* build a life with meaning. Believe it or not, making good money and doing good things in the world are not mutually exclusive. (Do you know how many homes Oprah owns? Six!) You can have it both ways. You can have wealth and success, *and* feel fulfilled and content in your work *and* have time to spend with your loved ones *and* look after your health. This is how my life is now. I feel totally fulfilled. If I were to die tomorrow, I'd be fine with that, because I'm spending my time on the things that really matter to me. I'm not sure Maddy would be okay with me dying, but you get my point — I don't have any regrets, and that's what I want for you too.

What Got You Here Won't Get You There

In the spirit of brutal transparency, if your life is not exactly where you want it to be right now, it's because your habits, your thoughts, your knowledge, and your actions up to this point got you this far, but they won't get you farther.

Jim Rohn says that to have more you must become more, and luckily, shifting away from where you are now to where you want to be in the future is relatively simple if you follow the steps laid out in this book.

It's simple, but not necessarily easy. It will take work and practice to master some of these skills. But the basics can be broken down into four stages and they make up the four parts of this book: Foundation, Clarity, Execution and Tactical Strategy.

FOUNDATION:

Foundation is about the mindset that you have to have, a certain way that you have to think and believe. This is about your conscious and subconscious programming. I didn't realize this until I left the nine-to-five world because I'd been so successful there. But success in a nine-to-five is very different to success as an entrepreneur, and so when I started my business, I realized that I needed to completely rewire my brain.

A lot of the clients we work with at High Impact Coaching want to become entrepreneurs, and the first thing we do is literally start unprogramming 20 to 30 years of mental programming. 95% of our brain is subconscious, and from the day we are born, that subconscious is being programmed by our parents and our environment to influence us to behave a certain way. Most of the time, society (which includes the education system we all go through, the media we all consume, and the governments that lead us) won't necessarily support your individual goals — and we'll get into why this happens in the next chapter. Society serves its own interests, and while we certainly benefit from living in society, the messaging we receive from it doesn't necessarily help on the road to entrepreneurship. But there are some key beliefs we've found in nearly all the successful people we've ever met, and we'll be digging into those in the next section.

CLARITY:

Once your Foundation is in place, we come to Clarity. You have to get clear on where you're going, and why. You can't get from point A to point B, if you don't know where point B is. Don't worry if you have no idea where you're going right now. Throughout this book we'll be doing a lot of work to help you build that clarity. This is all about figuring out what really matters to you, what really excites you and is going to set a fire under your ass. When you know *why* you're doing something, it's so much easier to figure out how you're going to make it happen.

EXECUTION:

Execution is about how you actually start putting what you're learning into action. This is about getting your habits and routines in place, so that you remove as much friction and resistance to your goals as possible. It's about creating a cycle of growth for you personally and for your business, protecting yourself against habit hijacking, and designing the right environment for yourself to work in, and succeed.

TACTICAL STRATEGY:

Finally, Tactical Strategy is about what to do and when: strategies for doing your most high-leverage work, learning the ropes of sales and leadership, understanding how to handle stress and anxiety, performing at your peak, and protecting your most important relationships.

But you need to remember that tactical strategies themselves are not enough. Why can two sales people at the same company — with the exact same scripts, training, and manager — get two different outcomes? They have all the same tactical strategy, but one might outsell the other by a factor of ten. It's because those two people can have two drastically different sets of skills, and mental programming (confidence, beliefs, habits) so they get totally different results. It's this combination of everything in this book that works like a combination lock. Until you have all the numbers in the right order, the lock won't open.

By the time you're done with this book, you'll be well on your way to becoming the entrepreneur or intrapreneur you want to be (and for the sake of simplicity, I'm just going to refer to both options as entrepreneurship for the rest of the book). You'll be shifting your mindset, starting to implement new habits, and bringing new focus and clarity to your work each day. So let's get going — first up, we're going to talk about some shit you definitely did not learn in college.

ONE

THE STUPID KID GETS SMART

"Knowing how to think empowers you far beyond those who know only what to think."

NEIL DEGRASSE TYSON

When I was in second grade, I did an IQ/aptitude test and the result came back in the bottom ten percent for my age. I had been struggling in school, and the report said I probably wasn't going to pass that year. My mom, bless her, was so loving that her reaction was, "It's okay! He's cute enough to make it without being smart." My whole family thought I was slow, and they loved me, so they didn't mind.

But my teacher, Mrs LaGrange, was having none of that.

After the IQ score came back, she held me back after class one day. She sat me down and looked me hard in the face. "Zander, do you want to be smart?" I looked back at her, and said yes. She smiled, and said, "Well, you're gonna have to work really hard at it".

I'm thankful for Mrs LaGrange every day of my life, because she implanted the idea in me, in second grade, that intelligence was not given. It's earned or it's learned. I worked really hard that year to learn how to read, to get better at math, and I ended up passing second grade, and third, fourth, fifth, and sixth grade without any issues. By the time I got to middle school, I was taking math at the high school. And by the time I got to high school, I was taking math at the local university. I finished all of my college math and physics classes before I even started at UCLA to do my engineering degree.

So my education in the growth mindset began when I was about seven years old. Mrs LaGrange made me understand that I had the power to change myself, even if other people didn't think I could. By the time I got to high school, I knew I could really do whatever I set my mind to... and since I'd figured out how to be smart, I set my mind to figuring out how to be social. I worked my ass off in class and I worked my ass off making friends. My mom let me have parties at our house, and if she ever caught on that I was skipping class, she never said anything. I had gotten so good at teaching myself from text-books that I realised that going to most high school classes was a total waste of time. I was getting straight A's in physics and math, and eventually convinced my teacher that if I continued to get A's, I shouldn't have to show up to class if I kept up the grades. My statistics teacher actually thought I had dropped out because I missed three weeks straight, but I was still taking the course — I was just getting someone else to hand in my work. Looking back, I might have overdone it a little — I almost wasn't allowed to walk at graduation because I skipped so many classes in high school — but I did the same thing in college. If you knew how to learn, going to classes was a complete waste of time.

In college, I was studying electrical engineering, I was the president of my fraternity, and I was in the Air Force Reserve Officer Training Corps (ROTC). I had a massive workload from electrical engineering, I had extra courses every quarter from Air Force ROTC (plus my Fridays were all spent doing drills and training), and running a fraternity is a full-time job, so I just didn't have time to go to class. I took what I had learned earlier in my life and figured out how to become far more efficient than what the general curriculum called for, and it showed: I graduated cum laude with a 3.5 GPA, despite not knowing what the inside of half of my classrooms looked like.

When picking up my final exam for one of my senior courses — I got the third highest grade in a class of 200 students — my professor asked me, "How come I have never seen you before?" I unapologetically told him it was probably because I'd only been there for two days of classes — the mid term and the final. He offered me an internship on the spot. And I had proof that doing things "my way" worked better.

By the time I got out of college, I knew two things:

1. that traditional education is extremely inefficient, and
2. that learning a bunch of stuff by rote does not prepare you for the real world. The seeds of Sh*t You Don't Learn In College had been sown.

What if I told you the education system you went through was designed to make sure you could never achieve your goals in life?

Would you call me crazy? A conspiracy theorist?

Well, let me prove it to you...

There are two types of education systems, and the one you went through is the wrong one for anybody who wants to get into entrepreneurship. That system — where you go through a set curriculum from early childhood until your late teens, and then go to college for a few more years — is what I call outcome-based learning. It's highly prescriptive and is designed to give everyone the same information at the same rate. It's faster for specific outcomes, but it tends to leave you as a "one trick pony". It's much better than nothing, but it doesn't prioritize teaching people how to think for themselves. It doesn't teach creativity, flexibility or critical thinking... which are kind of a big deal for entrepreneurs.

What I discovered after leaving college, though, was that the early Greeks had developed a completely different style of education, which was focused on creating successful, independent, contributing members of society. This was called the Trivium, and instead of teaching you what to think, it taught you *how* to think.

The three key components of the Trivium are Grammar, Logic and Rhetoric:

- Grammar is about learning how to learn on your own
- Logic is about learning how to reason and understand things on your own
- Rhetoric is about learning how to critically question what you hear, and effectively communicate what you know.

Sister Miriam Joseph wrote a book called *The Trivium: The*

Liberal Arts of Logic, Grammar, and Rhetoric, and she described it like this:

"Grammar is the art of inventing symbols and combining them to express thought; logic is the art of thinking; and rhetoric is the art of communicating thought from one mind to another, the adaptation of language to circumstance... Grammar is concerned with the thing as-it-is-symbolized. Logic is concerned with the thing as-it-is-known. Rhetoric is concerned with the thing as-it-is-communicated."

Another way to describe it is: knowledge (grammar) understood (through logic) and transmitted outwards as wisdom (rhetoric). Simply put, the Trivium's approach to learning gives you the tools for learning, so that you can figure stuff out on your own, and then share the wisdom that process has given you.

Imagine you are learning how to play the piano. You would start by learning how to read sheet music (grammar), then you would learn scales and how all the different notes work together (reason), and when you eventually mastered those two, you would learn how to critically think about the music you could play — maybe pieces by Mozart or Bach, or you could even create your own music (rhetoric).

Now imagine that you never learned any of this, but you were given a complex piece by Mozart and were shown the sequence of keys to press, over and over (rote mechanical repetition), until after a few months, you could play that piece by sheer volume of practice. But could you play a piece by Bach? Could you create your own music? No! Because you never learned the fundamentals, and that's the problem with outcome-based learning.

For an entrepreneur in the making, the trivium is a critical trio to master. When you can learn, problem-solve, and communicate, you're on your way to mastery of your craft, and mastery is what this is really all about. People would spend years, decades, mastering the three components of the Trivium, under the tutelage of other people. The model we have today, though, didn't come from ancient Greece. It came from ancient Rome, which was a highly militaristic, imperialistic society. It relied extensively on having soldiers, and what makes a good soldier? Someone who does what they're told, who doesn't question authority, and who never goes off-script because they've been thinking for themselves too much. If you want terrible soldiers, teach them to learn on their own, teach them to reason things out and seek out understanding on their own, and teach them to question everything they've been told. You won't build much of an empire, but you'll have a group of innovative and unique people who can propel society forward.

TRIVIUM VS. OBJECTIVE BASED LEARNING

TRIVIUM (Greece / Plato's Republic):	OBJECTIVE BASED LEARNING (Roman Empire):
1) Goal to create free thinking individual contributors for society.	1) Goal of creating "soldiers" or cogs in the wheel.
2) Spend years mastering the fundamentals (grammar, logic, rhetoric), before pursuing more specific topics.	2) Skip the fundamentals and focus on accomplishing a single outcome.
3) Mastery of the process of self learning, self reasoning, and critical thought.	3) Avoids mastery of self learning, self reason, and critical thought and builds reliance on the State for welfare.

Of course, the world we live in today is nothing like ancient Rome, or ancient Greece for that matter. The USA was founded on the importance of freedom — free thinking, freedom to learn and reason on your own, free speech — but the Industrial Revolution demanded a whole new generation of economic "soldiers", which regressed our models of learning back to that objective-based system from ancient Rome. Today, while most of us are not being channeled into soldiery or servitude, we are still taught to become cogs in a pretty specific wheel. We're still not taught to think for ourselves, and it's killing us. We *need* to master the skills of the Trivium, because without them, we become depressed, unfulfilled, unhappy, and sick.

Forbes did an article that found that 87% of all nine-to-five employees in the US are either unhappy, unfulfilled, or disengaged from their work.[1] Only 13% of 9-to-5 employees are actually happy doing what they do. That's crazy, right? That's one in eight people.

Anxiety and depression are all increasing every single year. Suicide is increasing every single year. Chronic illness is increasing every single year. And a majority of that is coming from stress, which is coming from a lack of fulfillment, a lack of purpose, a lack of alignment in what people are doing. When you spend 40 or 50 hours a week doing something that you're not aligned or happy with, it's only a matter of time before you become chronically stressed and actually sick. We're not meant to be cogs in a wheel.

Now, you can make the argument that this militaristic approach to education has allowed capitalism to progress to where it is today. Don't get me wrong: I'm a big fan of capitalism. All the advancements we've seen in technology, medical care, standards of living and so on are the result of capitalism. From a societal standpoint, having big corporations and organizations has moved the global economy forward very quickly. But there's no denying that has come at the cost of the individual. At the cost of people giving 20 or 30 years of their lives to a company, thinking they would be there forever, and then finding themselves out of a job, because that's what capitalism called for.

One of my clients at Cisco went through this exact situation a few months after I left. He was a senior vice president at a major media company, 55 years old with three kids, one of them in college, and he was let go one day without warning. He had spent 30 years in that place. It was part of his identity, all his skills were tied up in that role. And because he had never been taught how to learn on his own, how to adapt, he ended up completely lost. That man took his own life, because he was never taught what he needed to actually build a life on his own terms, instead of just doing what he was told. He struggled to find his way for months, and fell into a deep depression. Tragically he only saw one way out and I believe had he been taught the fundamentals of the trivium and learned to become a successful, happy, contributing member of society, things may have been different. A soldier without a rank is a lost soul.

I know that sounds extreme, but it's not uncommon. According to the Center for Disease Control, depression, anxiety and stress are at an all time high and suicide rates are up over 35% over the last two decades.[2] I don't want his story for you. I don't want you to get stuck in a situation where you're always at the whim of somebody else paying you, saying when you can or can't go on vacation, what you have to do with your time. I want you to be free to make your own decisions. I want you to call the shots on how you make your money, what you do with your time, what you choose to prioritise.

That's why this book is designed to teach you the skills of the Trivium — applied directly to entrepreneurship — so that you can build independence, self-expression, and a conscious career or business that helps you live in alignment with your dreams and values. It's designed to help you make more money, while having freedom and fulfillment to focus on what you really want. You're going to learn how to learn, how to reason out what's best for yourself as an individual, how to analyze and master your environment, to finally get results where it matters.

Read through this book in order. Each chapter and section will stand on its own, but it will be more useful to you in context. Occasionally throughout the text you'll find 'Comfort Crushing Challenges', which are designed to get you into action to actually start implementing the knowledge, because knowledge without implementation is worthless.

Knowledge can be your mortal enemy if you don't implement it. But knowledge with implementation creates wisdom, and wisdom is what leads to freedom.

Let's begin. You only get one life, and it's time to make sure it's a life you love.

---

1. *Forbes*, April 9, 2013, "Stressed Out at Work? It's Getting Worse, Study Shows", by Susan Adams.
   https://www.forbes.com/sites/susanadams/2013/04/09/stressed-out-at-work-its-getting-worse-study-shows/?sh=e8b8eb265de4
2. Centers for Disease Control and Prevention, NCHS Data Brief No. 362, April 2020, "Increase in Suicide Mortality in the United States, 1999–2018", by Holly Hedegaard, M.D., Sally C. Curtin, M.A., and Margaret Warner, Ph.D.
   https://www.cdc.gov/nchs/products/databriefs/db362.htm

FOUNDATION

Were you ever given an owners manual for your brain? I wasn't.

I got an owners manual for my new toaster. But not for my brain. Or my emotions. Or my body.

My parents did their best to explain to me how it all works, but they never had a manual either, so it was really just a best guess for them too.

Silly, isn't it?

How can we be expected to be successful when no one taught us how we work?

This foundational knowledge is what the Trivium refers to as grammar. It's understanding the basics well enough that you can figure out how to use them on your own. Going back to basics is about learning how to learn, how to utilize our brains, which is the most important tool we have. In fact, I call it the secret weapon. Obviously it's no secret that we all have a brain, but the secret is that the brain is far more powerful than most people realize.

You can use the space between your ears to accomplish

whatever you want. I tell everybody we work with that every person has some element of genius in them — most of us just don't know how to access that genius because it's been buried by all sorts of crap over the years. Most kids — about 90% — test extremely high for various types of intelligence at the age of 5, but by the age of 10, that number has dropped to 50%. By high school it's down to 20%, and by the age of 30, it's 2%.[1] So what's going on here? It makes no sense that we start life with the maximum creative genius we're ever going to have, right? What's actually happening is not that kids are not losing their intelligence as they get older, they're losing their *confidence* and their sense of what makes them unique. We all suffer an 'un-geniusing' process as we get older, through a rigid, one-size-fits-all education system, through careless comments from influential people that we internalise, and from all the messaging we're constantly receiving about what it means to be smart and successful.

So, how do you get back to really living your inherent genius?

Well, we need to re-genius ourselves. In my 2019 TEDx Talk, I shared research that suggests that 95% of your brain is subconscious.[2] Yep, I hate to break it to you, but you are in fact only 5% of a person. 95% of you is unconscious animalistic programing — ouch. Don't shoot the messenger! I didn't make you that way but I will help you to accept it: most people only have control over about 5% of what their brain is doing at any given moment. That's terrifying to a lot of people, but really, it's just evolution. While the brain usually only accounts for about 2% of our body weight, it consumes about 20% of our energy.[3] Humans are the only creatures in the animal kingdom with a brain to body ratio like ours. Our brains are huge, relative to other animals, which obviously gave us a lot of evolutionary advantages. But because it consumes so many calories — even when we're only consciously using 5% of it — your big ol' brain is an expensive piece of equipment. If you were consciously thinking about every single thing your body has to do to stay alive (like breathing, pumping blood, removing waste from your cells etc), your brain would need up to 20 times more energy than it already does. That is just not sustainable — we would die in a matter of hours if we didn't eat. We need most of our brain to be subconscious in order to minimise the energy we have to spend just staying alive. You're programmed to want to Netflix and chill. That would save your life as an ancient human, but now, it's slowly killing you.

So 95% of your brain is like a computer that's constantly being programmed. That's cool, right? Well, not if you're not the one programming it. If you're not programming it, who is? Well, it's mostly media, the community you live in, your family, your teachers — all the people and systems around you are always having an impact. And do those people and systems have your individual goals in mind? No.

Why is it important to understand all this? Imagine that you're in a cart, with five horses in front trying to pull you in the direction of your goals. These horses are thoroughbreds — the most badass horses ever. But at the back of the cart, there are 95 donkeys pulling together in the opposite direction. Who's going to win?

Your five horses might be strong as hell, they might be working together perfectly, but they're just never going to be able to overcome that resistance. The donkeys don't even have to be trying. They could be sitting lying on their asses chewing on grass and they would still outweigh the horses.

So: you've got to get the 95% of your subconsciousness pulling in the same direction as the 5% of your consciousness. Otherwise you'll struggle through your whole life, always wondering why you never seem to be able to get to where you want to go.

Training your subconscious to go in the right direction is how you start to re-genius yourself. That 95% has, for your whole life until now, been programmed by mass media, by your culture, by the people around you, but now it's time for your conscious mind to decide what programming goes in. For the rest of this chapter, we're going to get acquainted with the amazing piece of equipment that lives in your skull, and start to look at how you can train it to help you get what you really want.

1. TEDxTuscon, December 2011, "The Failure of Success", by Dr. George Land.
   https://www.youtube.com/watch?v=ZfKMq-rYtnc&t=329s
2. *New Scientist*, July 25 2018, "Lifting the lid on the unconscious", by Emma Young.
   https://www.newscientist.com/article/mg23931880-400-lifting-the-lid-on-the-unconscious/
3. *PNAS*, August 6 2002, "Appraising the brain's energy budget", by Marcus E. Raichle and Debra A. Gusnard.
   https://www.pnas.org/content/99/16/10237.full

TWO
YOUR BRAIN'S INSTRUCTION MANUAL

"Dreamers who never act and realists who never dream are the same. Neither end up with a life with meaning."

ZANDER FRYER

If Bezos, Musk and Jobs Had A Baby...

Did you know we have two operating systems running simultaneously in our brains at all times? Yep — there's an intellectual operating system and an emotional operating system.

What was your conditioned upbringing around emotions? Were you taught that feelings are weak? Unhelpful? Best avoided? Were you ever told not to cry, or to hide your emotions?

Our society is generally taught to run on the intellectual

operating system (which is sometimes called "left brain" thinking): a rational, data-driven, mechanical type of thinking. But a majority of our decisions and actions are generally dictated by our emotional operating system (the "right brain"): a more intuitive, feelings-driven, creative type of thinking:

- We say yes to working with people we like, because they make us feel something
- We buy products that evoke a feeling in us, either to escape a problem we have or to move ourselves towards something we want
- We don't date people because it's a "logical fit" — we date them because we fall in love.

Yet most of us are never taught how to handle our emotions.

People who are very left-brainy tend to be administrative or technical. Right-brainy types are more visionary. The left-brain is focused on the physical, tangible world out there. The right brain is more focused on the internal, imagined world. But when you combine the left-brain intellectualism and the right-brain emotion, you have a whole person. You get someone who's curious about what they could create.

The most successful people in the world are usually a perfect combination of both left and right brain. They're incredibly administrative, but also visionary. Think of Jeff Bezos, Steve Jobs, Elon Musk. They're great at being in the physical world, but they also have this imagined world where they spend a lot of time, and they're comfortable getting curious to see how they can join the two.

When you combine a desire for things to be measurable with a visceral feeling of curiosity or ambition, you get someone who's very inventive. If you take someone who is very logical and mix in strong intuition, you get creativity. When you find someone who's very linear and combine them with strong emotions, you get somebody who's able to heal their past and move forward.

There are a lot of people that are either just a bit more intellectual, or just a bit more emotional. The reality is that you want both. You want to be curious and inventive and creative and healed so that you can create the world you want.

LEFT VS. RIGHT BRAIN

LEFT BRAIN	RIGHT BRAIN	BOTH COMBINED
Administrative	Dreamer	Visionary
Measurable	Curious	Inventive
Logical	Intuitive	Creative
Rational	Emotional	Grounded

Unfortunately, for most of us, our emotional operating system and our intellectual operating systems are programmed in two different languages. Let's say the intellectual operating system is in English — we've all gotten very good at speaking that. But the emotional operating system is in Japanese, and so most of us are completely stuck.

Like I said, our society is highly intellectually driven, but society is made up of people, and people have lots of emotions.

he reason so many of us feel unhappy is that our
are constantly colliding with the cold rationalism of
and it feels incongruent and disorienting. No matter
what your preconceived idea of emotions might be — maybe
you think they're weak, unhelpful, chaotic, or maybe you think
they're useful clues about what matters to us — the reality is
that we all have them. We are not our emotions, but we have
emotions, and one of the biggest problems we face is that we
identify too much with our emotions. We make them part of
our identity, rather than something that can simply guide us in
the right direction.

So how do you learn how to understand and handle your
emotions better, without identifying as them? Well, first let's
start with how you identify emotions in the first place.

The two most powerful words in the English language are
"I am". Whatever comes after it directly programs that subconscious 95% of your mind and your identity as a person (more on
this later in the chapter). If I say, "I'm afraid", then my subconscious starts to identify as an afraid person, but I don't want to
be an afraid person! So I start to reject the emotion and do
whatever it takes to get away from that feeling. I turn off the
emotion in the 5% of my conscious mind... which means that
this feeling doesn't move through me, it gets stuck.

So where does it go? It buries deep down in that 95%
subconscious, and continues to run my life without me even
knowing.

Emotions are meant to move through us. The word 'emotion' comes from the Latin word, 'ēmōtus', meaning 'to move
out', and conscious resistance inhibits the process of moving
through an emotion. Emotions that you refuse to deal with are
the stem of nearly all 'limiting beliefs' or mental blocks. We all
have them — now we know where they are coming from.

So if instead I say, "I'm feeling afraid," I can acknowledge

that emotion without making it part of my identity. I can start
to work through the emotion, rather than fighting it. Letting it
move through me means that it resolves itself and my identity
doesn't get stuck on something I don't want. My subconscious
will get the message that something scary is going on, but it's
not going to cut and run when I need it to hold steady.

When you don't understand what's going on with your
emotions, you can try to figure it out intellectually as much as
you like, but there's still going to be that fundamental
language barrier. If you've shut off your emotional operating
system, you've also shut off half of your capabilities. This is
one of the most fundamental things that they just don't teach
you in college, but it's crucial to becoming both an
entrepreneur and a well-rounded human who is satisfied with
their life. So as we go through this process, I want you to try to
notice your feelings. Keep an eye on how each emotion makes
you feel physically, and when you feel something intense, get
curious about it. Don't try to stuff it down or ignore it. Start
learning your own emotional language, because it's absolutely
key to figuring out what you really want. It will keep you
going on this journey towards creating a bigger and better life
for yourself, and in the upcoming chapters, you'll find some
tools to help you work through the past stuck emotions and
mental blocks.

The Two Fears

Fear is the only reason we don't do all the shit we want to do. It
is literally the only thing standing between you and your
biggest dreams.

We're all born with two inherent fears: loud noises, and
falling. Loud noises can signal that something dangerous is
happening nearby and that you should get the hell outta dodge,

while the fear of falling keeps our little baby selves from crawling off a cliff when nobody's watching.

But that's it. The rest of our fears are self-fabricated, and by the time we get to being our adult selves, we are riddled with them.

We are the product of our evolutionary forebears, we have a completely disproportionate response to things we've learned to fear. I call this the "Saber-toothed Tiger Response". Fear is a very real physiological sensation. Let's say you hear something that scares you. For our ancestors, this might have been, say, a saber tooth tiger roaring nearby. For you, it might be the sound of your boss yelling nearby. The threat is completely different in scale, but the physical response is the same: blood rushes to your arms and legs, preparing you to run. Your eyes widen and your visual focus sharpens, so that you can spot the threat. Your neck stiffens so that you can look around you faster. Adrenaline pumps through your body so that you're ready to act in a split second, glucose is released into your bloodstream so you have energy ready if you need to fight or run. I'm not trying to gross you out, but your bowels get ready to evacuate in case your body needs to get lighter and therefore run faster, and the sweat you secrete changes, so that you would smell (and taste) bad to the tiger.

All this makes sense when there is actually a tiger nearby. But have you checked the bathroom for sabertooths recently? I couldn't find any the last time I looked. Your life is not at risk. You might be panicking that you sent that email to the wrong person, or freaking out because you missed a deadline, but these are not existential threats. These are socially-based fears, and we've learned them as a mechanism to keep ourselves in harmony with our social group. But fear always boils down to a fear of death.

Our learned social fears are ultimately a mechanism to

protect us from becoming outcast. As a prehistoric human, being outcast from your tribe meant death. Early humans could not survive alone — there were too many predators and environmental risks. Community is what kept early humans alive. Theoretically, the fear of death should be the biggest fear we have, but as a species, we've learned that our biggest fear should be the fear of judgment and shame. If your community shames you and casts you out into the cold, that's the most negative emotion we can feel, and Dr. David Hawkins talks about this in his book, *Power vs. Force*.

But again, we don't live in prehistoric times. We don't live in tribes of a few dozen people anymore. The existential risk of being outcast used to be that you would die, and quickly. Today, the risk of being outcast is, of course, psychological and emotional pain, but you're not going to die from it, and if we find ourselves cast out of one community, there's every chance that we actually find a better one as a result. Different communities are more interconnected and more inclusive than they have ever been before.

That means that our fears have a very limited utility. Our inherent fears of loud noises and falling can stop us from getting run over or falling off a mountain while taking a selfie, but there's not much else to it. So let's look at one of the most common fears people learn: the fear of public speaking.

Let's say you have never done any public speaking, and then discover that you have to get up on stage in front of 100 people and give the most important presentation of your life. You're terrified. What's going through your mind? *What if I forget my words? What if I stumble? What if I look stupid? What if I make a fool of myself and people remember it forever?* The fear is not necessarily about standing on stage with 100 people looking at you. The fear is about the potential outcomes of your talk. You're more worried that you're going to screw up your reputation, and then you're not going to get a raise, and then you're not going to get a promotion, and then you won't be able to have a nice home and give your family a good life, and that's going to bring shame on you, and then you're going to be an outcast and then you're going to die.

It sounds ridiculous when you see it all on paper, right? But this is what happens. You might not be consciously aware of all this, but it's going on in your subconscious, which shapes all the decisions you make and actions you take.

This is where fear journalling comes in. We've gotta dig down into that subconscious 95% and pull out whatever fears have been festering down there, so that we can work through them and then let them go.

Every morning when I wake up, the first thing I do is to search for the most negative crap that I can find in my brain and I write it out in a journal. I'll spend 10 to 15 minutes doing that. And if anybody found those journals, I would probably go to jail because it's some messed-up shit. I first learned to do this when my best friend, AJ, committed suicide, and all my worst fears came true. I realised that if I was ever going to get through that loss and move on with my life in spite of my fears, I would have to actually start dealing with them. A lot of people won't do this, because they're afraid to do it. People are afraid to look at the worst case scenario, to actually look at their scariest fears face on and really consider them.

This is contrary to what everybody says about the law of attraction and positivity, where you're supposed to just focus on the good stuff and hope the bad stuff leaves you alone. People sometimes ask me how the law of attraction works, and I tell them that the most important thing they can do is to learn how to sit with their negative thoughts. If you believe in the law of attraction, then what you focus on becomes your reality. I believe 100% in the law of attraction. My whole life is evidence that it works to bring amazing stuff into your world — so isn't it contradictory that I'm saying that you should focus on your fears? Wouldn't that bring your fears to life?

The short answer is no, because what you resist persists. If you have a crazy fear in that conscious 5% of your brain, and you refuse to acknowledge it, where does it go? It goes to your subconscious 95%... and you wonder why the law of attraction doesn't work for you. It's still there in your brain — you're just not thinking about it. But when you refuse to think about it, you also lose your power over it.

So the fear is still there. You're still feeling it in your subconscious, which means that you're exuding this fearful energy unconsciously... and then you're wondering why you're bringing crap into your world. It's because you're afraid to go and actually sit with that fear for five minutes and get it down on the page. The word emotion comes from the Latin 'emote' — "e", to eject, and "mote", to move through. You're meant to move through your emotions by actually experiencing them. If you can sit with your fear, acknowledge it, write it all out — it will leave you alone. But as soon as we reject an emotion or try to avoid it, it buries down into the subconscious and settles in (and you can read more about this in books like *The Body Keeps the Score* by Dr. Bessel van der Kolk and *Goodbye, Hurt & Pain* by Dr. Deb Sandella).

When you bring your subconscious fears up into your consciousness, you realize how silly most of them are. You will see how you can get past them, and allow yourself to let go of them. This is one of the most powerful exercises that I've done since I started my business. So grab yourself a journal (make sure no one else is going to find it) and see how many of your fears you can dredge up each morning. Go as negative and dark as you possibly can. Let yourself write out why these things scare you so much, and eventually you'll start to figure out where these fears are coming from and what you can do to let them go.

Connecting Your Conscious Mind and Your Subconscious Mind

Right now, you might be thinking, "Zander, that all sounds great. But how the hell do I get into my subconscious mind? It's subconscious!"

I'll tell you how in a minute. But first: can you feel your left foot? Can you feel the floor beneath your foot, and the warmth from your shoe or sock? What else can you feel?

I'll bet that before you read those questions, you were not consciously aware of your left foot. But as soon as I drew your attention to it, you started noticing all the physiological signals that your left foot is sending. Now, your foot is sending those signals to your brain all the time, constantly. It's how your brain knows that all is well in the Land of Left Foot. If all were not well, your brain would be receiving pain or discomfort signals, which would get your attention because it's a deviation from the norm. Your entire body is constantly sending signals to your brain, but you're not consciously aware of them until you turn your attention to a specific body part.

This process is controlled by the reticular activating system (RAS) — a bundle of nerves that acts as a filter between your conscious and subconscious mind. The RAS decides what makes it up into the 5% and what can safely stay down in the 95%. But your conscious mind can override the RAS, just as you discovered a moment ago when you consciously intercepted the signals coming from your left foot. The same thing happens when you decide, for example, that you want to buy a new Audi, and suddenly you see the Audi you want everywhere. There were always Audis on the road

— you just didn't notice them because you weren't consciously focused on them.

The RAS is basically the part that programs your brain about what you consciously notice and focus on, so when you learn how to program that, you start to be able to access that subconscious part of your mind and influence it in the direction you want to go. Maybe you've heard people say that if you focus on gratitude, more things come into your world to be grateful for. And that might be true, as I said about the law of attraction earlier. But it's also possible that your RAS starts drawing your attention to all the things that were already in your world, and which you're only just starting to notice and feel grateful for. When we program ourselves to focus on the positive stuff, we notice just how much good stuff we already have, and that creates an upward cycle of happiness and satisfaction.

How To Program Your Subconscious

Now that you know how powerful your subconscious mind can be when given the right information, it's time to get to work on actively programming it. There are two key tools for programming and reprogramming the brain, and those are repetition and emotion. The easiest way to implement repetition and emotion is through visualizations and affirmations — these are the concrete forms of repetition and emotion. Don't worry about exactly how to do them just yet. We will help you craft your own later in the section on clarity.

To do a visualization, you close your eyes and imagine what you want your subconscious mind to focus on. To do an affirmation, you repeat a phrase to yourself over and over again, so that it starts to sink into your subconscious mind, and we're going to take a deep dive on this in Chapter 5.

For the first year of my business, I had a million dollar bill I got on Amazon, and I posted it right above my laptop. So, as I was looking at my laptop all day long, I had a million dollar note sitting above it. This is another type of visualization. Even though consciously I was focusing on my laptop, subconsciously, I was absorbing the presence of a million dollars in my life all day long. Anything you can do to bombard your subconscious with the things you want — visually, auditorily or kinesthetically — will help program it to where you want it to be.

Regardless of whether you're a visual learner (you learn by looking), a kinesthetic learner (you learn by moving), or an auditory learner (you learn by listening), you want to find ways to repeatedly drive an emotional idea home to your subconscious using the method that works best for you.

If you're an auditory person, say your affirmations out loud. If you're a visual person, stick them up on the wall where you're going to see them all the time. If you're kinesthetic, write them out over and over.

I'm very auditory and kinesthetic (and you might have your own particular combination of what works for you). When I do my visualizations and affirmations each day, I'll stand up (kinesthetic) and get in a very powerful stance. Then I'll say the words out loud (auditory) which is very weird if you have neighbors and you're saying loud shit and the windows are open.

This is the same approach I take to journaling out my fears. I journal them by writing, not by typing, because I get more of that kinesthetic connection when I'm writing by hand. My wife is much more auditory, so she talks into her phone to 'journal' it out. Writing doesn't work for her, but talking through her fears, and then listening back to the recordings really helps her.

Any way that you can find to repeatedly drive a deep emotion home about a specific goal or idea is going to help you program that subconscious part of your mind.

The brain responds to deep emotion, and repetition. One of my favorite demonstrations of this is Pike Syndrome: a zoology study in Germany put a large pike fish into a tank with some smaller bait fish for a few days. Pikes are generally super aggressive hunters, so the little fish didn't last long. The next step of the study was to insert a clear glass pane into the tank, dividing the pike and the bait fish. The pike charged the smaller fish, ramming the glass divider over and over again, sometimes so intensely that it would be stunned for a few minutes. But after a while, the pike learned that it couldn't reach the bait, and it gave up. Even when the divider was removed, the pike didn't try to hunt the bait fish anymore. It had been so programmed by its environment that it lost its will to do the very thing it was made for.[1]

We are often just like that pike. We have some painful experiences that highlight a limitation, and consciously or unconsciously, we learn to just stay where we are. This is why reprogramming the subconscious is so important. You've got to pull out the glass divider in your own mind and start making moves!

Now, programming your subconscious is not a 'one and done' kind of activity. Some people say it takes 14 days to build a new habit, or 28 days to reprogram your brain, but the reality is that the longer you do it, the better the result you're going to get. 14 days will get you moving. 28 days will make you start to feel something. In 90 days, you'll see some big changes. A full year? you're a different person.

Let me tell you about how I visualized my way to a 7-figure business in less then a year.

Two weeks after quitting my 9-5, I was at a live event being hosted by my mentor, Jack Canfield. He invited me to get up on stage, and I leapt at the chance. I stood up there in front of 500 people and proclaimed that even though I was literally starting from scratch, I would be back at that same event next year, not as an attendee, but as a speaker. And as a speaker, I was going to be there sharing about how I just had my first $100,000 month in my coaching business.

I'm pretty sure some people laughed. Some thought it was "cute" that I had such big dreams. I don't think many folks believed it was possible.

I didn't even believe it was possible... yet.

But every morning when I woke up and every night before bed for the next year I closed my eyes and I visualized myself on stage telling the audience I had done it. And little by little my subconscious started to believe that it was going to happen.

Four months after that event, I was making between $10,000 and $15,000 per month. Within six months I was making $30,000 per month. Eleven months and 30 days later, I had made $90,000 in my twelfth month in business. Luckily it was July, which has 31 days, so I had one extra day to make it to my goal — and brought in $27,000 in clients on the 31st to round out the month at $117,000. Sure enough, Jack invited me back to the event to speak on stage, and I got to stand up there and say it all came true.

I still do my affirmations and visualizations every single day, and I've been doing it for years. I decided I wasn't just going to do this for 365 days and then stop, because what happens on day 366 if I'm not the one programming my brain? Who is? It goes right back to the external factors that are in my world that are programming me.

The brain is a muscle, and just like all your other muscles, if you don't use it, you lose it. If you program your subconscious every day, your brain stays strong and healthy. And if you don't train it, it starts to weaken. It's the same thing as being able to run long distances — if you train for it regularly, you'll keep being able to do it. But if you stop, even just for a few weeks, your capacity drops off drastically. So training your subconscious is a lifelong practice. Huge change can happen quickly once you get started, but you've gotta keep going to keep that momentum coming.

---

1. The Rainmaker Companies, December 13, 2018, "The Pike Syndrome", by Joe Fehrmann.
   https://therainmakercompanies.com/featured-news/the-pike-syndrome-2/

THREE
YOUR BELIEFS ARE BULLSH*T

"School is a great place to learn... but there are few if any classes on how to learn, how to think, how to remember."

JIM KWIK

The next step in building a strong foundation for yourself is to start to dissect the stories and beliefs you have about your life. Humans are story machines. We make sense of ourselves and the world around us through stories, both shared and individual. The stories we tell ourselves have a profound impact on how we view ourselves, and on what we believe we can achieve. Our beliefs are just the stories we tell ourselves, but they become our truth and our reality. Fortunately, we can create our own beliefs, and discard the ones that don't serve us anymore. In this chapter we're going to dig into what those beliefs and stories look like and how you can make sure they're serving you.

The Cycle of Outcomes

I remember when I was ten, and I wanted to jump off the high dive board at the swimming pool. All these stories were running through my mind. "I'm too scared to jump off! I'm going to break my leg, and then I'm going to die because I'm going to drown with my broken leg and nobody's going to save me because I'm gonna look like an idiot!" (It all comes back to those fears of being outcast or dying, right?)

But did I climb back down? Did I go find my parents and say, "Dad, please! I need to go to therapy to fix all these stories I'm telling myself"? No! Eventually I ignored those stories for what they were — illogical fears that were stopping me from having fun. I jumped anyway, and it was so fun that when I surfaced in the water, I felt like I could do anything. So of course, I ran back up and did it again.

The stories we tell ourselves are powerful, and they're totally within our power to change. Either we control them, or they will control us. Tony Robbins always says, "You have to fix your belief" — that the motivation and inspiration has to come first before the action. And he is right, but it's only part of the equation. We always need to be working on our beliefs and changing the stories because they control most of that 95% of our subconscious. But sometimes, all you need to do to get a different outcome (and change your belief at the same time), is to take the action that scares you. Jump off the high dive. My belief before was that I was going to die if I jumped. Afterwards, it was nothing but joy and excitement.

The fastest way to overcome a fear is not to try to undo the 95% programming that's making you scared. It's actually just to do the damn thing that scares you. If you want to overcome more fears, do one thing that scares you right now. It doesn't matter what it is. Are you afraid of doing a Facebook Live? Grab your phone, do one right now. Doesn't matter where it is, doesn't matter what you talk about, just do it. You don't even have to do that if it's too much — just film yourself on video and start taking steps towards it. Just do one thing that makes you uncomfortable, to start building the habit of getting uncomfortable, and then it starts to snowball.

When you create a different story, it gives you a different feeling, and your new feeling leads to more action. Now you're creating momentum. We call this the Cycle of Outcomes:

THE CYCLE OF OUTCOMES

In the upper left corner, you can see that the cycle is kicked off by an event. Something happens. The 'something' is actually neutral — there's no such thing as a positive or negative event. Think about this. Let's say the New York Jets played the New England Patriots in football last weekend and the Jets beat the Patriots. If you're a Patriots fan, you tell yourself that's a negative event. You feel shitty and maybe drink too much and then get in a fight with your wife. But if you were a Jets fan you tell yourself that was a positive event. You feel elated and happy and maybe you go propose to your girlfriend!

Can you see how the event itself can't be both positive and negative? The event itself is neutral, but our story is what makes it a positive or negative experience for us individually. Even something as horrific as the 9/11 attacks is neutral. Sure, to you or me, it was an absolute tragedy. But were there people — even if just a small group — somewhere in the world that celebrated it? No doubt about it.

The story you tell yourself about the event leads to a particular feeling, and the feeling will usually trigger an action. And because it's a cycle, the action will often trigger another event, and the whole thing starts again, and depending on whether your story is positive or negative, this can create an upward spiral in your life, or a downward spiral. There are two points at which you can intervene in the cycle: either changing the story, or changing the action. Changing your actions is a pure act of will power — just do it! (#nikeswoosh). But changing the story is where you really start shifting your beliefs and that subconscious 95%. We are going to give you the tools to intervene at both of these points throughout this book, because when you have the power to control your stories, your feelings, and your actions, you have the power to control your outcomes.

The Belief Hierarchy

We are born completely free of beliefs. We are blank slates, but over time, we start to internalise the beliefs of the people and community around us. Between the ages of three and eight, we start to form beliefs about the world, based on what we're told by our parents, grandparents, teachers, other influential grown-ups and the media we consume. Even though our beliefs might not be particularly sophisticated at that young age, these beliefs start to form the foundation of our future, and each belief either supports us or detracts from us.

The first thing to figure out about your beliefs is whether they are true. So are they? Are your beliefs actually true? Or are they bullshit? Whenever we coach a new group at HIC, I ask this question. Usually about 50% of people will say yes, the other 50% say, "I don't know". But let me ask you — have you ever had a belief that turned out not to be true? Of course you have. At one point in time, everybody believed the earth was flat, and that it was at the center of the universe. Beliefs are our best guess about what's true, based on the information we have at hand and our emotional landscape. They're not objectively true, but they become our truth. Understanding your beliefs and how they affect your view of the world brings clarity and action (or inaction).

It's my belief that you're a good person, and that as a result, your inherent desires are for the good of this world. My belief is that your desire to get more out of life, to create more wealth and freedom and meaning — that's all good. That's the story I believe about people like you, because I've seen the proof play out in the real world many times. That means that any belief that's holding you back from those goals is getting in the way of helping the universe become a better place.

And if my belief *is* true, and you *are* a good person and you *do* want to have a positive impact on the world through your personal journey, you have to make a conscious choice that whenever you find a belief that's not serving you, that you will rip it out by the roots and replace it with a belief that does... and don't worry, I'll show you exactly how to do it.

There are three levels of beliefs in the human brain.

At the very fundamental level are your core beliefs. These lead to your identity beliefs, which in turn lead to your general beliefs. These three levels tend to dictate the stories we tell ourselves, the thoughts we think, the actions we take, and eventually the outcomes we achieve.

1. Core Beliefs

We usually have two or three core beliefs that drive all our other beliefs. These are the beliefs you have about "universal truths". My core beliefs are that nothing is fixed and that the purpose of life is to grow, that good always wins over evil, and that I am responsible for everything in my life. These core beliefs free me from the fixed mindset that "This is how I am and that's that", or "God made me this way and I can't do anything about it". It gives me the power to choose what I want my life to mean.

2. Identity Beliefs

These are the personalized versions of your core beliefs, influenced by the environment around you — what you deeply feel to be true about yourself. My personalized identity beliefs are that I can grow and become whatever or whoever I want to be, that I have a responsibility to do good in the world and not to let evil sneak in around me, and that I take 100% ownership of everything I do. Personally, I believe I am a good person, a student of life and a great leader. I am strong and confident and always make decisions from a place of love and purpose, not fear. Can you see how these identity beliefs almost guarantee my success in life? What if I believed I was a terrible leader and a shitty person. Would I be writing this book?

3. General Beliefs

Your identity beliefs shape your general beliefs, which shape your actions. For me, my general belief is that I'm better off as an entrepreneur than I was in my nine-to-five, and that no matter what happens, I'll be able to figure it out. I also believe this book will change your life because of my identity as a student of life and all the knowledge I've gained, so I have to get it into the hands of as many humans as possible. I believe my clients will achieve all of their goals because of my identity as a great leader.

Belief Breaker 8 Exercise

But what do we do if we don't have strong beliefs, or good identity and core beliefs?

"Zander, am I screwed?"

Don't worry. I'll feed you, baby bird.

There's a process I call the Belief Breaker 8 (lovingly nicknamed BB8, for all the Star Wars fans). This is a set of eight questions you can ask yourself that will help you eliminate any negative beliefs that are not serving you.

Remember when you go through this exercise that beliefs are not reality. Beliefs are stories that we tell ourselves, and these 8 questions are a combination of some psychotherapy techniques, and some deep coaching techniques to essentially help you unprogram and reprogram your beliefs.

(And a quick side note: we've compiled all the exercises in this book into a free e-workbook to help guide you through them — be sure to visit www.sydlicbook.com and download it to make working through each one easier.)

Beliefs are the habitual thoughts that we think so often they become reality. So if you want a different reality, take ownership of your beliefs and change them so they serve you. It's like taking a knife, and grinding it around in a piece of wood until the groove gets so deep, you almost can't pull the knife out (or you don't even realize that the knife just keeps going around in a circle).

Question 1: What's a belief that you have that is holding you back?

Don't worry about whether this belief is objectively true or false. Just think of a belief you have that is holding you back. We all have them, but sometimes it can take a minute to identify them. Let me give you an example. In the coaching space, it might be, "I can't charge $3,000 for my services." I hear this all the time. We've worked with hundreds of coaches, from 18-year-old college dropouts to yoga instructors, to stay-home moms, primary school teachers, you name it. There are hundreds of different reasons people in our programs believe they couldn't charge $3000 for their coaching services. But as soon as we show them this belief is not true and doesn't serve them (and give them some sales frameworks), they start enrolling clients at $3000, $5000, or even $8000 per month.

Question 2: How has this belief benefited you in the past?

The reason we create this belief is because there is some form of benefit to us. Normally it has something to do with creating a sense of safety, comfort, or self-preservation. Maybe the belief that you can't charge a lot of money for your skills protects you from having to learn the scary skills of having sales conversations. Maybe it protects you from upsetting people in your life who don't earn much. Maybe it protects you from dealing with a more painful belief, that you yourself are not worthy of abundance and joy. Maybe it prevents you from having to try and potentially hear a "no" — remember fear of social rejection (or being outcast) is as strong as the fear of death.

Question 3: What is this belief costing you now?

When you figure out what this belief is costing you, you're going to get really motivated to get rid of it. Students often realize that their belief about not being able to charge a lot is what's preventing them from making money in their coaching business, it's preventing them from getting out of their nine-to-five, it's preventing them from getting clients, it's preventing them from helping dozens, hundreds, even thousands of people, and it's preventing them from getting the real transformation they deserve. When you get really clear that the benefit of this belief was to keep you safe — but actually all it did was keep you small — then you realize the drastic cost to yourself and all the people whose lives you could potentially change.

Question 4: Do you want to keep this belief?

The answer to this question should always be no. If the answer is yes, you want to keep this belief, then stop the exercise here. But I can't imagine you would want to keep such a limiting belief once you've figured out what it's really costing you. And at this point, we've pulled the knife out of the groove and you're no longer deepening that belief. You've consciously realized that belief does not serve you and it is just a lie. Acknowledging that and making a clear decision that you don't want to keep it lays the groundwork to start changing it.

Question 5: Can you think of a time when this belief was not true, either for you or others?

The next thing we want to do is to start to create a new equal belief in the opposite direction that does serve us to replace this old groove. If you think you can't charge $3000 for what you're offering, are there other people charging that much? You can bet your ass there are. Ignore the little voice in your head that says, "Yeah, but they're more qualified/famous/cool than me". Doesn't matter. Is someone else doing what you want to do? Then you can do it too. It might take work, and you might have to practice some new skills, but you can do it if you really want it. Let's say you think you can't be successful as an entrepreneur. Have you been successful in other things in your life? What are some areas in your life where you have been successful? Can you think of a time that this old belief was not true for you or for others, so that you can really kill that old belief and completely disintegrate it?

Question 6: What do you really want to be experiencing?

The answer here might be that you want to be able to enroll clients at prices, like $3,000 or $5,000, consistently and confidently, and you want it to feel natural, and not to feel like a sleazy sales pitch. That's what most of our clients really want to be experiencing. Our beliefs are like the blueprints to reality, so we have to start to create a new belief for that new reality to start to come through.

Question 7: What is the belief that would support the new reality you want?

At this point, the new belief might be, "I can enroll clients at $3,000. People are ready and willing to pay $3000 or $5000 for my service. My service is worth $50 grand, so charging $5,000 is pennies compared to the transformation my clients are going to get. When people work with me, their whole life is going to be changed. And at the end of it, they're gonna say I undercharged them." These are the beliefs that you need to start to create.

Question 8: What are 1 to 3 affirmations that will solidify this new belief?

Create 1 to 3 affirmations, just as bullet points, that you can put on a note card, and read to yourself when you first wake up, when you go to bed at night, and multiple times throughout the day to start to reprogram this belief.

Let me share a story about the belief that nearly took my entire business down.

The first three months of my business were crazy, as it always is when you start a new business. But I got the hang of it, and after another few months, things were really humming. I was getting plenty of clients, people were getting results, and money was coming in. I had gone from making nothing as a coach to bringing in over $30,000 per month within six months.

And then my best friend AJ killed himself.

We had been best friends since we were in elementary school. He joined the Marines straight out of high school, and struggled with post-traumatic stress, anxiety and depression his whole life. In spite of that, he was the lightest, funniest, silliest person you've ever met. He constantly inspired me. But there was this really dark deep pit inside him that he tried to keep away from everybody else, and in the end it consumed him.

I had worked with people with PTSD, I had worked with

people with suicidal tendencies, depression, trauma, and I had been trying to get him to work with me. But because we were close, he wouldn't. I could see what was going on with him, and I kept throwing out the life raft, but he kept resisting. He didn't want me to feel responsible for him in any way.

Remember how we talked about emotion being a powerful way to program your subconscious? Well, when you have a deeply traumatic emotional experience, like your best friend killing himself on your watch, it creates a very, very deep groove in your mind. It's like somebody took a plasma cutter to that wood we talked about before and just dug it straight in.

I started to believe that if somebody worked with me, they could die. That I was a fraud. How could I pretend that I was going to help people? How could I lie to people and tell them that I was going to help them, when I felt like my failure had the potential to kill every single person that I was working with? I didn't even want to get on the phone with people. Now, I knew logically that all this was not true. I knew logically that it didn't make any sense. But it didn't matter — my intellectual operating system was still intact, but my emotional operating system had exploded.

This was the groove I was stuck in, but eventually I realized that I had to figure out a way to reprogram these beliefs, these stories, which are deep seated in my emotions, and my subconscious mind, to be able to continue to move forward. I knew I would never be able to sell coming from that sort of pain and negativity. And if I couldn't sell, then thousands of people were not going to get my help. So I had to figure out these deep-seated beliefs, and rip them out one by one. Deep down, I knew there were people out there that needed me. And I knew that all of these fears, this need I had to feel safe, everything I just created, was preventing all of them from getting what they needed from me. I started going through the Belief Breaker 8, and I did it multiple times. By the end of it, I had a list of about 10 different bullet points that I was clinging to for dear life.

Here's what it looked like.

"What's a belief that's holding me back?"

Well, I don't want to get on the phone with people because I'm a fraud. I don't want to do a sales call because people are gonna pay me money and then they could commit suicide, based on the things that I'm going to walk through with them.

"How has this belief benefited me in the past?"

It's prevented me from feeling pain. It's kept me safe from the agony of losing my best friend. I never want to go through an emotion like that again. It's protecting me from having a situation like that over again. It's self-preservation. I'm in a world of depression and anger and angst and turmoil. I don't want to feel this, I just want to feel any sense of normalcy.

"What is it costing me?"

It's costing me my business. I just quit my job and it's costing me my life, my purpose, my passion on this earth, if I don't figure this out. I can't go back to a 9 to 5. And I have to figure this out. And on top of that, it's costing hundreds, potentially thousands or even potentially millions of people in the future, if I can't figure this out. I know that I could reach millions and millions of people in the future. And if I do not get rid of this belief, those millions of people will never get the benefit of the work I'm here to do in this world. Plus there are millions of dollars in my future that will not come my direction. This one belief could cost me tens or hundreds of millions of dollars, depending on which direction I take in the future.

"Do I want to keep this belief?"

Hell no. No way.

"Can you think of a time that this belief was not true?"

Absolutely. I'd helped dozens of people already. I'd helped dozens of people, including other people with PTSD, trauma and terrible setbacks, and they had all gone on to live, and to be much happier, more fulfilled and at peace than before I had worked with them. I had seen how I could help people first-hand. So I knew this belief was not real, that this belief was not true.

"What do I want to be experiencing?"

I want to be able to get on the phone and do sales calls, but also feel like I'm connecting with people and helping them and having fun. I want every conversation to feel like I was changing somebody's life for the better. I want to feel like I can do this again. And I want to have a belief that my programs and my services really work, and that they are exactly what everybody needs.

"What beliefs do I have to create to support that reality?"

I combined this question with "what are the 1 to 3 affirmations", and created a mass of bullet points. Things like:

- "I love doing sales conversations".
- "It's just an opportunity to meet a new friend and change their life".
- "These people need me and without my help, they will be stuck in their hell."
- "This is never about me, it never was, and it never will be."
- "I am strong enough to fight through whatever fears come up for me, because I know that people out there need me, and my help is life changing."

I read these every single day for months and months until they literally replaced my old beliefs. When I was learning how to do sales, in this time period of deep depression, I never wanted to handle objections, because as soon as somebody gave me an objection, I crumbled. It was like them just hitting me right in the heart of losing my best friend, like they were telling me that I wasn't good enough.

So I added another belief: "I love objection handling. It's an opportunity to coach someone through their fears. It's the best coaching session they'll ever get, and they haven't even paid me yet". I didn't realize how powerful it was until about six months later when I actually met the woman who would become my wife, Maddy. She was watching me on the phone with a potential client, and she could tell when somebody came up with an objection, because I would smile. A huge smile would come across my face, no matter what the objection was, because I knew this was my moment to shine as a coach. My belief now was that this was my moment to help somebody make the crazy change to bet on themselves and transform their life. That's the power you can have too when you commit to cultivating the right beliefs.

Comfort Crushing Challenge #1

Go and get five hugs from five random strangers. Ask five people that you don't know if you can have a hug. If that sounds easy to you, then the alternative is to go out to dinner alone. Don't take your phone. Just be there in your own company. One of these two things will make most people very uncomfortable. Do the one that makes you more uncomfortable.

If you can't physically hug people, then you could give five random people compliments, or start a random conversation with five people in public. Watch the stories that go through your head as you do this. "Will people think I'm weird? Will people say no? Will it be awkward?" Who cares!

One of our students was a guy who lived in NYC, and he said he was certain that if he asked enough people for hugs, someone would punch him in the face. Instead he ended up with five people who felt so warmed by the gesture that he ended up staying in Central Park for the rest of the afternoon handing out hundreds of free hugs. The story in his head had nothing to do with the reality of the situation.

FOUR

THREE KEY BELIEFS FOR SUCCESS

"Life is hard when you want it to be easy. Life is easy
when you expect it to be hard."

BEDROS KEUILIAN

Tony Robbins says success leaves clues. So if I want to have
successful beliefs I would just model the beliefs of the most
successful people right?

Well, over the past several years I have worked with
hundreds of entrepreneurs and had the pleasure of (both infor-
mally and formally) interviewing hundreds of seven-figure
earners, eight-figure earners, and even billion-dollar business
owners.

I have found there are really 3 common core/identity
beliefs among the most successful people in this world, and
these are the three fundamental beliefs we want to start to
program into your brain as you get started on your journey of

building a life with more money, more freedom and more meaning.

Belief #1: Full Ownership

Taking full ownership for everything in your life is about becoming the victor of your own story, rather than the victim. Arnold Schwarzenegger says, "You can have results or excuses. Not both." I totally agree with him. Jack Canfield — author of the bestselling *Chicken Soup for the Soul* series, serial entrepreneur, and one of my closest mentors — says that to truly succeed, you have to take 100% accountability for your life, meaning everything in your life is there either because you create it, or you allow it to happen. This is a jarring idea for a lot of people, because bad things happen to us that are outside of our control. There's no denying that. But you need to take 100% responsibility in your life, and at the very least you need to pretend that you are 100% responsible and accountable for everything in your life. Because there are things that are outside of our control, but if you think you're, say, 80% responsible for your life, what happens when something doesn't go your way? That always falls into the 20% that's "not my responsibility." It becomes very easy to blame and complain and make excuses about other things. But as soon as you take 100% accountability, responsibility, or what I refer to as full ownership, you stop being the victim, and you start being the victor. Whatever comes your way isn't always what you want. But you can take any circumstance, and you can control your thoughts, you can control how you feel about the situation, which then dictates your actions and outcomes. That's 100% ownership.

Your life of more money, more freedom and more meaning starts with taking full ownership. It's an acceptance that you are the adult in the room. Nobody else is going to save you. You're not a kid anymore. Your parents aren't going to help you get the life that you want. The President is not going to help you get the life that you want. Nobody is going to hand you the life that you want. So if you don't take ownership over your life, nobody will.

Taking full ownership is scary. It means that everything is on you. But the upside is you finally have the power to change things. Whatever circumstances come your direction, you end up having the capability of overcoming them, rather than making excuses. When you don't take full ownership, when you decide that something is out of your control or that there's nothing you can do about it, you're giving away your power. You're throwing away the possibility that you have the ability to respond and change the situation. But as soon as you take ownership, you can act, you can change, you can move things.

When you blame somebody else for your situation, or you make an excuse about why it's not your responsibility, you're giving the power to somebody else. The most disempowering thing that you can do is relinquish your autonomy like this. There's no way you can ever achieve the life that you want if you give the power to somebody else. If you never take full ownership, you will never accomplish anything. It's all up to you.

As you go through this book, we will give you the tools to overcome what's in your past. Maybe you've had something go wrong, or you were dealt a tougher hand than most from the start. But the reality is that if you're here, looking for ways to change your life, then you're conscious enough to fix those past problems or to find the tools and support that will help you do it. And the truth is, somewhere out there, someone with the exact same excuses as you, rose above them to change their life. You can do it too, once you take full ownership.

You might have limiting beliefs. You might have traumatic

experiences in your past that have caused those beliefs. But like we've talked about, you can unprogram and reprogram your brain. If you take responsibility for unprogramming and reprogramming your subconscious, you literally have the tools to overcome those limiting beliefs, to overcome those past traumas. But you have to own that fact.

There's a difference between explanations and excuses. Explanations let you understand how you got to where you are. Excuses let you *stay* where you are. Remember: You can have results or excuses. Not both.

Full Ass Only

A soccer coach told me in high school never to half-ass anything, always go full ass. If you always go full ass, you'll never have any regrets.

If you half-ass something and say you gave it your best shot, that's an excuse for not going all in because of the fear of failure or judgement. You can tell people you gave it your best shot, and maybe they'll accept that, but you'll know the truth, and you'll never get what you really want until you go full ass.

Albert Einstein once said that "Great spirits have always encountered violent opposition from mediocre minds."

And let me tell you, he was right. When you start going full ass, it scares people. It scares them to see you go for something they're too afraid to do. Understand this. Most people go through life half-assing everything, and when you start going full ass, it's going to trigger their deep fears and insecurities. It's going to bring all their limiting beliefs right up to the surface when you start breaking through your limitations.

I don't like to sugarcoat it. You will lose friends. When that happens, you'll know that, frankly, those people shouldn't have been in your life anyway, but I'm not going to tell you it doesn't hurt. It does. It can make you question yourself and what you're doing. But you are the average of the five people you spend the most time with. So if you hang out with five smokers, you'll become the sixth. If you hang out with five people who are broke, not going anywhere and fixate on negativity all the time, you become the sixth. If you hang out with five people who are millionaires and doing amazing things and impacting the world and saving lives, you become the sixth.

I couldn't tell you how many friends I lost when I quit my job and started this coaching business. I always group them into the 3/3/3 Rule. They're either a three-day person, a three-hour person or a three-minute person.

As I started to really go full ass on this new life, I realized when I was in the nine-to-five, there were people I would hang out with for three days straight for an entire weekend. We'd go drinking and party hopping and doing all this stuff. But I realized I had to downgrade a lot of those people to a three-hour person, where we might catch up for a drink or dinner, or maybe even a three-minute person, where I would have a quick conversation with them on the phone, but I wasn't going to spend a weekend hanging out anymore. I had the world to change! I had other shit to do, and soon I noticed that there were people who had previously been three-minute people who were actually really positively minded. They were motivated. They were doing things with their lives. They quickly turned into three-hour people and even three-day people.

So yes, you'll lose some people. That's okay. You'll find new ones, and they'll lift you further than you can imagine right now.

And as I upgraded, my community upgraded, and the people that I had to downgrade, they were watching. And they started to upgrade too because they saw how things were changing for me. Some of them tried to pull me down, and when I didn't get pulled down and I kept going, they said, "Well, if he could do this, I could do this. Maybe I should start stepping up. Maybe I should start changing". I didn't have to pull them along with me. They were watching me go full ass, and it forced them out of their comfort zone.

The same thing happened to Maddy when she started going down this path of personal development and spiritual development. She wanted to share everything she was learning with her family, to bring them all along with her. At the beginning, they weren't interested. They didn't want to hear about it. But over the next few years, as she grew and grew and became even more awesome, her family started to go full ass too, because they saw how much her life has changed for the better. She didn't have to do anything. She didn't have to drag anybody with her. It's a slower process this way, but you can either be a lighthouse or a tugboat. Being a lighthouse keeps you shining. Tugboats are constantly down in the muck and the drama. Be a lighthouse.

5% More Ownership exercise

This one's from Jack Canfield. You go through the different areas of your life, and you ask yourself: if you could take 5% more ownership for this part of your life, what would you do?

Let's say you were looking at your health and wellness. Grab some pen and paper and write this out: "If I were to take 5% more responsibility for my health and wellness I would..."

Then list out three to five things you could do. Maybe it's to drink more water, or get to sleep before midnight. Maybe it's going to the gym three times a week. Just be honest.

Next write out: "If I were to take 5% more responsibility for the accomplishment of my goals I would..."

Then list out three to five things you could do.

Repeat this for your financial situation, your relationships and any other part of your life that you want to improve. List out three things you could do in each area that move you closer to full-assing your effort in that part of your life.

A lot of people think they're already taking full responsibility for everything in their lives. But when you ask them where they can take 5% more responsibility, they'll be able to list something in every section. How can you be taking full responsibility if there are things you can take 5% more responsibility for? It's uncomfortable to realize, but the fact that you can find something in each area means that you're not taking 100% responsibility.

(And don't forget: you can grab the free e-workbook to help guide you through these clarity exercises on the website: www.sydlicbook.com.)

Belief #2: You're Not Good Enough

I'm gonna tell you something that no self-improvement guru will ever tell you. You're not good enough. If you were good enough, you'd be where you want to be already. But the truth is you're not. Which is why you aren't. Now before you yell "blasphemy!", let me expand a little.

You're not good enough... yet. But you can become good enough.

In her book *Mindset*, Carol Dweck describes the difference between the fixed mindset and the growth mindset as being the single biggest contributing factor to someone's success.. If you believe you come into the world with a specific set of abilities and there's nothing you can do to change them, that's a fixed mindset. But if you believe you come into this world with a specific set of abilities that you can develop and grow, that's a growth mindset.

I believe we are all given some form of natural ability, but that we're also given the ability to learn and grow. Like I told you before, in the second grade, I was the slow kid. But I learned. I developed intelligence. Most people think that intelligence is a natural thing, something innate or God-given. But I'm living proof that you're not stuck with what you were given. It took years, but I developed enough intelligence to surpass even the naturally bright kids.

There's this idea in the self-development world that you're already good enough. Personally, I think that's damaging. I think it's harmful. Because it stops you from trying to do more, to become more. It gives you an excuse, it gives you an out. But one of the most consistent things I've noticed in having this conversation with hundreds of people that are successful in every part of their lives, every one of them has actually accepted that they're not good enough. And that is actually okay, because they know they can become good enough. Jim Rohn says, "if you want to have more, you have to become more."

Understand that I'm not talking about your inherent worth as a human being here. I'm talking about your skills and abilities. As a human being, you're already a masterpiece. You're already worthy of love and safety and happiness. You have worth and you have a destiny, you have a purpose in this world. But part of the purpose is growth. Nearly all of us can improve our skills and abilities in every part of our lives. Your skill set is not good enough yet, and to get to where you want to be, you need to work on that.

You can be a masterpiece and a work in progress at the same time.

The Purpose of Life

You don't need to meditate under a lotus tree for decades to learn the purpose of life. I'll tell you right here: the purpose of life is to grow.

Some say it's to love. Some say it's to serve others. Some say it's to live your purpose. In the end all of these things require one thing, and that's for you to grow — emotionally, mentally, spiritually, and to become a better person as a result.

We start with a basic set of capabilities, and our job is to grow them and use them and change the world for the better with them. It's not easy, but since you're working towards your life's purpose, I think the juice is worth the squeeze.

John Maxwell says that "Growth is discomfort, discomfort is growth." You can't have one without the other, so becoming the person you need to be is going to take work and effort. Upgrading your skills and abilities, upgrading your emotional intelligence, your ability to deal with your own stuff — it's hard. Growth is not fun, and if you think it's fun then you're doing it wrong. Expect growing pains.

So, what counts as growth? Growth requires taking knowledge and putting it into action in order to create wisdom. Think of it like building your muscles. How do you build your muscles? You have to put them under tension. You have to put weights on them and stress the muscle over and over and over again, while making sure that you're putting the right stuff into your body. Over time, the muscle is built. It's the same with psychological and emotional growth. Do hard things over and over and over again, make sure you're putting the right stuff into your mind, and your abilities will grow.

Growth requires action. That's why just reading a book is not necessarily growth. Books can set you on the path to growth, but without action, it's knowledge for knowledge's sake.

Knowledge without action is not power. Knowing stuff is not the same as growing, and it won't lead to wisdom. Even this book — you can read it cover to cover, you could memorize every word, but if you don't put what you learn into action, it's just a waste of time. 100% knowledge multiplied by 0% action will get you nothing.

The Fear of Shame and Being Outcast

This particular cocktail of fear is one of the primary reasons that people don't grow into who they could be. It's a symptom of the fixed mindset. Let's say you inherently believe that you're a 5 out of 10 at tennis. You really want to play in your local competition, but to get in, you really need to be an 8 out of 10. Well, if you're a 5, and you have a fixed mindset, you're not going to try to get better, because you might fail. And if you fail, you think you can never try again, because what will people think of you? Obviously they're doing to judge you, criticize you for failing, mock you — right? Everybody knows that you're a 5 out of 10 tennis player and you'll never live it down.

The fixed mindset doesn't allow you to consider that failing once just shows you where you are right now, so that you can start to work on getting better. Once you know where you are, you could get lessons and maybe work your way to being a 6, then a 7, then an 8 out of 10 tennis player, and maybe by next season you'd be ready to join the competition. The fixed mindset doesn't allow you to consider that literally nobody else gives a shit about how well you play tennis and that the requirement for the competition is just there to control the number of players in the competition. It doesn't allow you to see that maybe not being amazing at tennis yet doesn't mean you're a failure who deserves to be banished to the wilderness, doomed to be forever alone.

I'm exaggerating now, but do you see how ridiculous that is? This applies to every part of your life. You might think you're a 5 out of 10 on the scale for romance, or fitness, or intelligence. But there are *always* things within your control that you can do to budge that number and start taking some control of your life. And believe me — even if some people don't want to see you succeed, there will be plenty of others who appear to cheer you on.

Now, the fixed mindset doesn't just apply to negative things. While in high school, I actually went from having that growth mindset to a fixed mindset because one year I didn't show up to physics class at all, then took the exam and aced it. I got 96%, and everybody started to refer to me as "the genius who doesn't have to study"... and I developed a mindset that if I had to work hard, that means I wasn't a genius any more. I was afraid of ruining my reputation as the genius who doesn't have to study. But I had studied — just not in class — and so I ended up paralyzed by this fear. I felt like I couldn't study, couldn't work hard, but I knew if I didn't that my reputation would end up shot anyway. I got really stuck here until I realized that it was okay for smart people to work hard too.

I think that most of us are on a spectrum between the extremes of totally fixed and totally growing mindsets in different areas of our lives. In your business, for example, you could be of the growth mindset at a level 9. But in your relationships, you could be of the growth mindset at a level 2. You could be really open to being uncomfortable and growing in your business, but not so open to growth and discomfort in your relationship, or in your physical health. It's a spectrum, and our job is to gradually inch our way up the scale in every part of our lives.

Become More

At this stage I want you to close your eyes (well, maybe read this section and then close your eyes at the end). Envision yourself 10 years from now accomplishing everything you've ever wanted: you have all the money you've ever wanted, you have the career you've always wanted, the relationships you've always wanted, the health and wellness you've always wanted.

Think about 10 characteristics that you would need to embody in order to get to that stage and accomplish your dreams. Ask that version of you if you want to, or just start listing out what comes to mind. Maybe that future version of yourself is courageous, maybe they're honest, maybe they're patient, faithful, diligent and so on.

Then I want you to score yourself on these qualities. On a scale of 1 to 10, where are you now?

Finally, write down one thing you could start doing that will develop each quality. If it's honesty, what's one thing that you could start doing? Don't lie about your weight, or how much sleep you really got, or the time you actually left your house to go meet your friend. Choose something simple like that, to help move yourself forward on each quality, so that you start becoming that person you need to be *today*.

Belief #3: Have A Little Faith

Jim Carrey once said: "Take a chance on faith — not religion, but faith. Not hope, but faith."

Faith is a bit of a taboo subject today, but having interviewed hundreds of successful entrepreneurs in the past few years, I have not met one that does not have some form of faith. And, like Carrey, I use the word faith very specifically. We're not talking about religion here. We're talking about belief and trust in something bigger than yourself.

If we are being totally honest, entrepreneurship is illogical. It doesn't make sense for anyone to do it if you think about it too realistically. To succeed in entrepreneurship and choosing this new life for yourself, you have to have some form of faith that there is a better life waiting for you. Whether it's faith in god or Mother Earth, or universe juice, or multi-dimensional aliens that look out for us, you have to believe that good is the prevailing energy in the universe. I call it the Disney principle: believing that ultimately, good defeats evil, and that if you're a good person, things will go right for you. I watched a LOT of Disney movies as a kid, and those movies programmed my subconscious so powerfully that I have always believed that good prevails, love prevails.

And because that belief supports the outcomes that I want to create in life, I attach to that belief with every fiber of my being. I'm not religious, I'm not sure I believe in God, per se, but I do believe there's a higher consciousness, something bigger than all of us, something that unifies everything, because there have been too many positive things happen in my life for me not to believe that.

But whether or not this belief is true, I don't really care. It doesn't really matter. That belief supports me, it helps get me to where I want to go, it helps me be happier. This is a belief I've actively chosen, and I'm going to keep it.

The Alcoholics Got It Right

Every time a chapter of the Alcoholics Anonymous meets to support each other, they finish the meeting by saying the Serenity Prayer together. If you're not familiar, here it is:

God, grant me the serenity to accept the things I cannot change.

The courage to change the things that I can,

And the wisdom to know the difference.

I first learned this prayer after my DUI when I was 21 years old (and we will get to that story later). I thought it silly because I didn't believe in "God". But over the last five years of really diving deep on what it takes to be successful, the more I realized something profound. The alcoholics got it right.

There is a reason that AA is one of the longest standing self-development organizations in the world (it was originally founded back in 1935). This whole prayer is about faith, and relying on something greater than yourself to help you do what needs to be done. The very first part of the prayer is about having faith that you will find the serenity to accept the things you cannot change. The second part is about having faith that translates into courage to take action (which goes back to taking 100% ownership).

This is a balancing act. Our logical brain thinks, "How can I take 100% responsibility and have faith in something bigger than me at the same time?" Learning to handle that paradox is what faith is all about. You have to be 100% an owner of your life, and at the same time, you have to have faith that it's going to go the right direction, even when things are not fully in your control.

There are things that you cannot change. You cannot change a past outcome. You cannot change the actions of others. But you can change how you react. You can change the story you have. You can change what you do in the future. And that's what faith empowers you to do.

Just before I graduated college, I got a DUI, and I knew, as soon as it happened, that the DUI would get me kicked out of the Air Force. I'd had three beers, had never drunk and driven before, and I thought I would be okay, just this once. But as soon as I got stopped at a DUI checkpoint I knew I was wrong. I had spent over five years training and developing myself as a leader for the military. I was a leader in my detachment, I scored top marks in everything I did, and I graduated top of my class at Field Training (AirForce ROTC's version of bootcamp). I won the "Top Gun" Award, and was on track to train and fly fighter jets (I wanted to fly F22s). And here I was sitting in the drunk tank, a fraction over the legal limit, asking myself, "Why did this happen to me?"

That created such strong feelings of resentment and guilt and frustration that I started crying my eyes out. All I had ever wanted to do was serve, and I had been on track to start flying F22s as a fighter pilot. After I got done bawling, I realized I was asking the wrong question. Maybe instead of asking why it happened to me, I should be asking why it happened *for* me. People always tell you things happen for a reason. Maybe that's true; you never know when you're in the thick of it. And at the time I had no way of knowing whether it was happening for a reason, but at that moment I decided to have faith that something bigger was going on. And look where I am now. I'm not flying F22s, but I run a multi-million dollar company that is helping me to serve on a totally different scale.

Had I not gotten that DUI, I would be halfway through a twenty-year career commitment in the AirForce, with little to no control over my life. To this day, I regret that I was never able to serve my country. But I can't deny that I am better off because of it.

So now I'll ask you to reflect and do the same. Think back and list out three "rock-bottom moments" you've had in your life. Maybe it was a DUI like mine? Losing a loved one? A tough breakup or a divorce? Not getting the job you really wanted? A traumatic injury?

Whatever it might be, I bet (in hindsight at least) that you can think of at least one good thing that came from it. Realize that in some way (sometimes a very weird way) it happened for you — not to you.

Fear vs Purpose

After I quit my job, it became clear that I wanted to become a coach. I spent a ton of money investing in different programs, masterminds, and coaching. After three months I was still not making a dime and was now $25,000 in debt. I'd maxed out both my credit cards, and in about three weeks, I had to pay rent. I was not sure at all that I would make rent, but I was pretty sure that if I didn't make rent, I would be out on the street. One day I got a call from one of Cisco's partners, offering to pay me $10,000 a month, just to put me on their roster. Literally all they wanted me to do was make introductory emails to connections I had from my Cisco days with people at companies like Disney, NBC and Facebook. Ten grand a month for some emails.

I drove home from the meeting with the contract on my lap. *Damn. 10K sounds pretty good right now.* But I knew that I had to ask myself the hard question: Am I making this decision out of purpose or out of fear? The answer was scary, but it was true. I wanted to take that job out of fear. I was afraid that I couldn't make it happen for my own business in the next three weeks. I knew I already had everything that I needed. I just needed to actually sell something.

I didn't sign the contract, and I went to bed that night feeling sick. But I knew it was the right thing to do. Two weeks later, I enrolled my first client at $3,000. The next week I enrolled a $4,000 client. The week after that I enrolled a $6,000 client, and so that month I brought in $13,000. I have never been so happy to pay rent in my life. I paid all my bills and started paying off my credit card. The next month was $17,000. Then $24,000. Then $32,000. Then $44,000. The rest is history. But that was a pivotal moment in my life, and it's all because I chose to have faith in my purpose rather than to let myself be sidelined by fear.

Nobody else can tell you whether you're making decisions out of fear or purpose. Sometimes it's easy to tell yourself it's from purpose, but you'll always know, deep down, if it's really out of fear.

As much as humanly possible, we want to make our decisions more from a place of purpose than a place of fear. The only way that you can make a purposeful decision is in the face of fear. It takes courageous action to make a purposeful decision, and the only way you will make a purposeful decision is if you have faith that it will turn out better. This is putting it in the terms of your emotional operating system. To put it in the terms of your intellectual operating system, you have to learn to take risks, and to back yourself. Most people never learn to take risks and the logic and rationale that they think is protecting them is actually holding them back. Being completely rational, following social norms and cultural logic will keep you stuck. You have to be a little bit irrational to accomplish big crazy things, and operating from a place of purpose helps you get past all the rational fear and desire for comfort that would keep you from accomplishing anything at all.

So I got really good at making the scariest decisions I could possibly make every day.For the first year, every single day when I woke up, I did the one thing that scared me the most. Every day. I called it my "Big Cajones Action." It didn't matter if it was business related, relationship related, health, and wellness related, because I knew I wasn't good enough yet. And I knew that to become the person that deserved a seven-figure business, I would have to grow, and I knew if every day I did the thing that made me the most uncomfortable, I faced the most fear, and I took the most purposeful action, I would reach my goals. I knew if I made uncomfortable decisions in all those different parts of my life every single day, I would grow enough to become that person I needed to be.

So I said no to that contract. I called up an ex-girlfriend and asked her to give me feedback on our relationship. That was the most uncomfortable conversation of my life. Do you know how terrifying it is for a man to call an ex-girlfriend and ask how he was in bed? So cringeworthy. But I got so much great feedback that I guarantee that conversation is the reason I'm so happily married now.

I am a total mama's boy, but I called my mom and told her she couldn't call me, she couldn't come see me for the next six months, unless I reached out to her. When I quit my job, she thought I had all kinds of free time, so she would call me or comve visit all the time. I told her, "I need you to understand that this is gonna be the most crucial 6 to 12 months of my life. And I need to be focused, so I can't just be hanging out all the time." That was a hard one. My mom is Pakistani, and all my Indian and Pakistani friends freaked when I told them. "What?! Did you get smacked in the face?! You can't do that to your mom!" But she did what I asked, and our relationship got even better.

Practicing Gratitude In A Drunk Tank

Remember when I told you about that moment in the drunk tank when I realized I was getting kicked out of the Air Force, and the plan I'd had for the next 20 years of my life went up in smoke? Well, not only did that moment teach me to ask how a situation might be happening for me rather than to me, it also showed me how to have gratitude in the mud. It taught me that one of the most important skills in life is to be able to find a way to be positive in real shitty situations, and this is where your faith enters the picture. If you have faith that what you're going through right now is a stepping stone to that next thing, or that it is an important turning point in your story that's going to lead to a positive ending, that's gratitude in the mud.

When you truly, deeply have faith, when you believe that things are happening *for* you, if you believe that good wins in the end and that everything you're going through has a purpose, you're always going to find a way to overcome your challenges and suffering. And so you start to handle (and maybe even enjoy) a lot of the shittier things that you go through in life. You know it's just going to make your story that much sweeter by the end. Think of your life as a movie: when somebody watches the movie of your life, you want it to be a damn good story. And a good story isn't all daisies and rainbows —you have to have the pit of despair, and you have to go through that stuff to come out the other side.

My buddy Vince Del Monte uses the analogy of a grape seed. The grape seed is destined for greatness. It's destined to become a beautiful, sweet fruit., and then that sweet fruit is destined to become a beautiful vintage wine, one of humanity's most sought-after delicacies. But how does the grape seed start its life? By being buried, deep in the earth. It's cold, it's dark, there's no way out. The grape seed has to fight to come up out of the ground and finally reach daylight. It has to fight to grow into a vine and finally gets to create delicious, beautiful fruit. But just when it's reached this pinnacle, all the fruits of its labor are taken away and crushed. The grapes are stripped from the vine and crushed into oblivion, then cramped up in a big dark space again. If you were a sentient grape seed, and you didn't understand what you were destined for, this whole process would absolutely suck. It really would. But if you know you're destined to be a beautiful fruit, and then you're destined for another stage of growth, which is becoming a beautiful vintage wine, then you would know that this process is worth it. All the change, all the 'setbacks' — they're all just steps along the way to becoming what you're meant to be.

Facing Your Fears

Here's an exercise you can do to start moving yourself from fear to purpose. List out ten things from this last year that you chose not to do out of fear.

You might tell yourself that there was nothing you didn't do out of fear... but after having worked with nearly a thousand people on this exercise, I have never once had someone who was completely void of fear based decisions. Dig a little deeper and be a bit more honest with yourself.

Maybe you didn't apply for a job, you didn't tell your partner something because you were afraid of how they would react, or not speaking up in a meeting. Don't write down any reasons or justifications for why you didn't do these things: just put down ten things — big or small — that you know you didn't do out of fear, and then write down how you felt after the opportunity to act had passed. When I do this with clients, they say things like "I felt ashamed, like I'd let myself down. I felt like a coward, and I regretted not doing it."

Then write down ten things that did, in spite of being afraid. Maybe you did apply for that job. Maybe you did have that tough conversation. Maybe you did speak up. The difference here is to write down how you felt about each of those things after doing them. When I do this exercise with clients, they say they felt accomplished, motivated, proud, lighter, happier and braver.

Any time you've ever done something scary you will always feel motivated, energized, brave, and proud. Courageous action breeds more courageous action. Now: we're nearly through building your foundation. There's just one more thing you've gotta get your beliefs around.

You're Going to Die.

The day I lost AJ to suicide was the day I truly started to live.

One day he was here. I could talk to him. I could hug him. I could smack him when he pissed me off. And the next day he was gone... forever.

He sent me one last text the night he hung himself. "I love you man. You have so much greatness in you." I sent him one back. "Thanks brother! I see it in you too man. That's why we are on this journey together."

No response.

The next morning when I saw his dad calling, I knew. I knew he was gone even before Papa Tony told me.

Now was the hard part. I had to accept the fact that my best friend was dead. And that meant that I had to accept that one day I would die. That we will all die. Obviously I struggled for months. I spun into a deep and dark depression and constantly questioned everything about my beliefs and my own reality.

But in that grief, in that loss and heartbreak I started to feel a shift. In the darkness it was the small lights that started to shine bright. The jasmine flowers outside my window never smelt so amazing. Hugs from my friends and family never felt so energizing.

And the more comfortable I got with death, the more I started to live.

This is not a new idea: the acceptance of death is a big

feature of a lot of philosophies and religions, especially Stoicism. If you accept death, the way that you live becomes very different. While I was working on this book, a quote came to mind from the book *Tuesdays with Morrie* by Mitch Albom. One of the main characters, Morrie, says that everyone knows they're going to die, but nobody believes it. If we did, we would do things differently — and I can't think of a truer way to think about it. We all know we're gonna die, but none of us truly believe it. It could happen in a week, it could happen tomorrow. We will die eventually. And when you get to that moment — to the very last day that you will live — how do you want to view your life? In every study and interview with the elderly, the two biggest regrets are not taking bigger risks and not building stronger relationships with their loved ones.

Entrepreneur and author Ed Mylett talks about this moment of moving on to the next world: he says that when you meet your maker, and your maker shows you what your life could have been if you lived your highest purpose, you want to recognize that person, and know them very well, because you were that person. I think when you start to live life with this understanding of death — accepting that your death is inevitable — and live with the intent of being able to look back on your life and see that you took important risks, that you loved people deeply, that you lived purposefully, that really changes the way that you act.

Now, I know this is uncomfortable. Death still feels taboo and too scary to talk about. But at some point you're going to be forced to accept it. I was forced to accept it when AJ died. Some people still won't accept it even after being forced into that kind of situation. But for me, when AJ took his own life, it really sent me into a whirlwind of figuring out what life was really about and what was really important to me. I realized that it can be taken from you or it can be taken from a loved one in an instant, and that's it. There's no coming back from it. I was forced to go into deep contemplation and to really unpack what I believed about death.

Frankly, there's no way to know if what I believe is right, or for you to know that what you believe is right. But I don't really care. I choose the beliefs that serve me. And what I believe is that we should live as though karma is real: don't be a dick, because what goes around comes around. Your purpose is to live purposefully, to grow, to bring more good into the world. Make the right ethical decisions, be courageous, give more, be more grateful, act from a place of love and gratitude. I think if we do that, we'll get to our last day on earth and be satisfied with the story of our life.

Comfort Crushing Challenge #2

Let's say you live a long, healthy life. You meet your maker (or end up floating through space as stardust again) as a result of natural causes. You're shown a movie of what your life could have been if you lived your highest purpose.

1. What would need to happen while you're alive for that movie to be the life you lived?
2. List out what you want people to say about you at your funeral.
3. Think about what they would say if you died today, compared with what they would say if you died of old age, having lived your highest purpose. Would they say the same things?
4. If not, what needs to start changing to make that happen?

CLARITY

Alright! You did it! You learned some fundamental beliefs, and figured out how your brain and emotions work, so now you've got the foundation in place, and it's time to get to work on clarity. Because if you don't know where you want to go, how can you ever expect to get somewhere you really want to be?

Getting clarity about where you're going in your life — and with your business — is a crucial first step. That might sound obvious, but getting clarity on what you should be doing with your life is a lot like a jigsaw puzzle. When you have all the pieces, you can see the whole picture. If you have most of the pieces, you can figure out what's missing. Even if you only have some of the pieces (say, 30% of the puzzle) you can still see a bit, and start to decipher things, and then it only gets clearer as you keep moving. But most people are running around without *any* pieces of the jigsaw puzzle in place... but they still expect to just find themselves in a life that they want to live. It's not going to happen if you don't have clarity. If you don't know where you want to end up, how will you ever figure out how to get there?

Everybody walks around wondering what decisions they need to make in order to make their lives better and easier. Life is a series of decisions, either purposeful or fearful. But you can't make any useful decisions at all if you don't know what you want and what's actually going to make your life feel meaningful. This is why the exercise about getting comfortable with your own death from the end of the last chapter is so important. If you know how you want things to end — how the movie of your life plays out, and how people remember you — you're providing a little bit of clarity as to how you should be acting now. You can work your way backwards to how you need to be making decisions today.

You might have a few pieces of the jigsaw puzzle in hand already. It may take a lifetime to collect every last piece, but you're job from this point out is to start picking up every piece you can, and intentionally working towards getting clear enough to make smart and purposeful decisions each day.You're not going to find them while you're writing emails at work, or taking out the trash at home, or making a presentation at work. When you're in the minutiae of daily life, there's no opportunity to stop and look around at what you're actually doing. You need to regularly carve out time and energy to specifically start thinking about what you really want, whether you're on the right track to get it, and if not, how you're going to adjust course to get there. In this section we're going to go through a whole selection of exercises that will help you start to put the pieces of your clarity jigsaw puzzle together. I do all these myself every six to twelve months, to make sure that I'm refocusing and every time I'm getting a little bit more clear, a little bit more concise.

FIVE

DO WHAT YOU LOVE

"Do what you love is for amateurs. Love what you do is for professionals."

SETH GODIN

When I first quit my 9-5 I told everyone I was retiring. When they asked what I meant, I'd say, "When you do what you love, you never work a day in your life."

Man, that was stupid.

Three months into my business, when all my savings had dried up, I was forced into a harsh reality. There was a lot more to this entrepreneurship thing than just "doing what you love"... especially if you wanted to make money while doing it.

It was time to learn how to love what you do.

The truth is, if you want a life with more money, more meaning, and more freedom, the direction that you should pursue is normally a combination of three things: what you want, what you're good at, and what the world wants and is willing to pay for. This is the Clarity Venn Diagram:

CLARITY VENN DIAGRAM

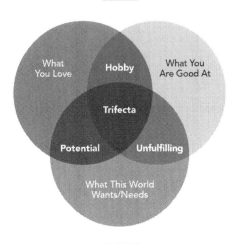

For most of us, work takes up about 40 hours a week (and for lots of us, 40 hours is the bare minimum). It's about a third of your waking hours. So if you're going to be working that much of your time, you better make sure that it's something that's aligned with who you are as a person. Choosing your career is a crucial part of building that life where you have more money, more meaning and more freedom. Getting this right is key to the whole 'more money' part of the equation.

So you want to enjoy it. Then, obviously, you want it to be something that you're good at, because most of the time, you're not going to get paid good money for something if you're not good at it. And lastly, it needs to be what the world both wants and is willing to pay for, because you won't be able to build a profession, career, or business out of something, if nobody's gonna pay you.

In this chapter we're going to focus on how to figure out what you want to do and what you really love. In the next chapter, we're going to focus on what you're good at and what you can get paid for, but first, I want to take a second to define money. I'm not being an ass, I know you know what money is, but most of us have a lot of head trash about money, which makes it really hard to make a lot of it.

Money Defined

All money is just a physical or digital placeholder for social value. If I want to buy a flight from United Airlines and I can't provide United a service they are willing to trade for, I have to give them money, to transfer them the equivalent amount of value I will receive for taking the flight. If you bring value to somebody, they pay you money. If you bring more value to somebody, they pay you more money, you bring more value to more people, more people pay you more money. To make money, you have to provide something that the world wants and values. Doing what you want to do and being good at it is not good enough. Let's look at some of the configurations here.

1. If you are passionate about something and you're good at it, but the world won't pay for it, you can't make a career out of it. It could be a hobby at best.
2. What the world wants and what you're good at is also not enough. This is what I fell into when I was at Cisco — I was providing a service that the world wanted, and I was damn good at it. But it wasn't what I wanted. I made great money for years, but I

was unfulfilled and unhappy, like there was a big hole in my life. That happens to a lot of people, and they end up filling that hole with alcohol, sex, sports, video games, constantly traveling — anything to distract themselves and make themselves feel whole for a little while. That's what happens when you go after something you're good at and this world wants, but you don't truly love.

3. If there's something that you want, and the world wants, but you're not good at it, that's actually okay to start at — if you are willing to put in the work you can *become* good at it (growth mindset baby!) and get to that beautiful trifecta point.

This is what we're going to focus on getting clarity around for this section of the book. The exercises here are the reason I was able to quit my job at Cisco on the spot to start my business. I had worked through them all so many times that I had so much clarity and one day just realized I was done, and that I couldn't rightfully and intelligently continue to work at Cisco when it was so clear that it was not in alignment with my purpose.

Why It's So Hard to Find Clarity

It seems like figuring out what you want out of your life should be easy. But it's really not, and that's because for most of us, our subconscious has been programmed not to allow ourselves to want anything at all. We're taught not to be selfish, we're taught not to ask for things, we're taught to prioritize what other people want. When you were selfish as a kid did your parents praise that? When you were vocal about your own desires, was that encouraged? For most of us, the answer is no. Of course, there's a lot of utility in teaching children not to be selfish. But it's often taken to the extreme, where kids are actively discouraged from freely expressing their own needs and desires, and then we wonder why they grow up to be adults who feel suppressed and depressed. It's the same thing with bragging. In my opinion, bragging is one of the most important things you can do, because your self esteem is built by acknowledging your accomplishments. You don't have to go on and on about yourself, but you do have to be able to talk about what you've done and to be proud of yourself. If you're not going to brag about yourself, who is? I mean, my mom is amazing for this, she would brag about me all day long, but if I had to take my mom with me everywhere, that would be really problematic. I have to celebrate myself, because that builds self confidence, which builds self worth, and self-worth allows you to acknowledge and pursue what you really want.

There's an exercise I love to help break down the subconscious barrier that is stopping you from really getting what you want and being able to celebrate that. It's called 101 Wants.

101 Wants

The goal of this exercise is just to write down 101 things you want to do, be or have in this life. It's like a bucket list of stuff that you want to achieve or acquire or experience. Sounds simple, right? Well, yes, it is simple, but for a lot of people, simple is not going to mean easy, and if that's you right now, that's okay. The reason this exercise gets difficult is that as we list out all the things we want, we find a way to talk ourselves out of it.

Here's an example:

#17: I want a million dollars.

Actually, no, that's going to be too hard to pull off. Too big, what am I thinking? Maybe I should just write down $100,000 instead.

Booooo. Do you see how quickly you can justify not wanting what you want? I'm not saying you have to pursue everything on your list. All I'm asking you to do here is an experiment — an exercise in acknowledging the fact that you have needs and desires, and getting comfortable with what they are. So: what do you want?

Allow yourself to dream here. Get rid of all the restrictions and all the reasons you can't or shouldn't have what you want. Just allow yourself to want stuff. Just for the duration of this exercise. It can be anything. Here are a few ideas:

- A million dollars (obviously)
- Big house with a garden
- Two kids
- A month-long trip to Madagascar
- Weekly art classes
- Original collector's edition of Star Wars figurines
- Two months of vacation every year
- Pay off my parents' mortgage
- Start my own successful business
- Get front row tickets to the SuperBowl
- Adopt a shelter dog
- Buy a farm
- Compete in the Cooper's Hill Cheese Rolling Race
- Camp in the backwoods of Colorado
- Retire at 45
- Be so spiritually developed that I can move shit with my mind (like a Jedi!)

There is no end of possibilities to what you might want. Grab your notebook or a piece of paper and take some time right now to start working on your list. It's okay if it takes you a few sittings to get all the way to 101 things (it took me two 45-minute sessions the first time I did this. The only rule is that you can't talk yourself out of wanting anything, for any reason. No excuses, no justifications, no "I only get one week of holiday per year", no "my parents would never forgive me", no "that's too dangerous/hard/risky". Just want what you want and write it all down.

(If you need somewhere to work through this, make sure you head to www.sydlicbook.com to download the free e-workbook.)

Following Your Joy

The Dalai Lama says that if you're ever unsure where to go, use your joy as a compass. The reason I want you to get so comfort-able with wanting what you want is that following your joy is one of the fastest ways to clarity. And usually if you're having trouble figuring out what brings you joy, the answer is on the other side of fear. Ryan Holiday talks about this a lot in his book, *The Obstacle is the Way*. This is a key principle from Stoicism: the thing that is difficult, the thing that opposes you is the direction you're meant to go. Joy is so often directly on the other side of the scary thing that you're thinking about that if you ever have trouble finding your joy, you can actually follow your fear. It seems weird, but it works pretty damn well, because joy and fear are not on opposite ends of the spectrum. Joy is on the other side of fear. You have to face your fears to find your joy and purpose. When you go through that transfor-mation, you get extreme clarity. And once you have extreme clarity, fear has less and less hold over you. You're so crystal clear about what you want and your greater purpose that it becomes almost impossible for you not to move forward. It becomes more uncomfortable to stay where you are than to move forward.

Here's the next exercise, to help you get some practice at following your joy:

Take 10 minutes to write down 20 things you love to do. Don't think about it too much. It could be anything. It could be taking the dog for a walk, hugging, kissing your spouse, having a glass of nice tequila, eating pizza and burgers, hanging out with friends, reading a good book, teaching little league, whatever.

If you're having trouble with this, then think about the last time that you lost track of time. What were you doing that got you so immersed? List out 20 things. Once you've got your 20, go back through and spend another five minutes listing out why you love each one of these things.

Let me show you: I love to hug and kiss my wife because I love connecting with her. I love a good glass of tequila because I love just being present in the moment and relaxing and letting everything slide off. I love reading a good book because I love to learn. I love to travel because I love to explore new places. Pretty straightforward, right? Just a quick reason that you love each thing.

Once you're done with listing out why you love each thing, go back and start looking for themes. I have done this exercise with over a thousand people, and everybody has three to five paradigms that run through their life. These are the themes that dictate the things that you love to do, they are markers for your joy. The goal is to find these three to five paradigms. When you find them, you can start to design a life that allows you to have more of the joy they create in your daily experiences. Around

80% of your life should be focused around these three to five paradigms.

FIND YOUR JOY

Step 1: List 20 things you love to do (in left column below)
ex: I love travelling, I love reading, I love spending time with family, etc.

WHAT	WHY
1. Drinking nice tequila	I love being present and grounded
2. Spending time with Maddy	I love connecting with others
3. Reading a good book	I love learning and growing
4. Traveling to new places	I love getting a new perspective and learning
5. Coaching clients	I love teaching and serving others
6.	
7.	
8.	
9.	
10.	
11.	
12.	
13.	
14.	
15.	
16.	
17.	
18.	
19.	
20.	

So let's say you love hiking. Why do you love it? Because you love to explore new things. So, you're not trying to design your life around hiking (though that will feature). You're trying to design a life around exploration. You're focusing on the function, not the form. Or maybe you love reading. Why do you love reading? Because you love to learn and grow. Again, you might not design your life around reading specifically, but maybe you can start to design a life or a profession that requires you to learn and grow constantly. The goal of this exercise is to look, at the surface level, at 20 things you love to do. Then you distill it down into why you love them, and then from that you find the three to five deeper functions. I love to learn, I love to teach, I love to be present, and I love to deeply connect with people. And you can design a life around those three to five things that truly bring you joy. When you focus on the function, it frees you up to find more and more forms of that joy.

The first time I did this exercise, the paradigms I identified were that I love to learn, I love to connect with people on a deep level, I love to teach, and I love to be present in the moment. I asked myself, what percent of my life right now do I live in accordance with these four joys? The answer was about 20%, which was terrifying. But if you were to ask me that question today, I'd say probably between 90 to 95%. Being clear on what brings you joy can be your compass to the life that you need to live.

So that's the first part of the exercise. The second part is where it gets really wild. This is where we take your joy and use it to figure out your life's purpose.

First, we start with three basic questions about yourself.

1. First, ask yourself: what are the two traits that make you different from everybody else? It could be your drive and your creativity. Or it could be your empathy and curiosity. Whatever they are, write them down.
2. Next: how do you enjoy expressing these personality traits with others? Maybe you love inspiring and empowering others, or you love caring for people and going deeper in your relationships.

3. Finally: what would your idealized version of the world look like? If you got to make everything just as you wanted it, how would people behave? How would they interact? What would the environment be like? What would be happening?

Then you take all your answers and stitch them together into a single statement of about 15 to 20 words to figure out what your life's purpose is. Then spend some time refining it until it absolutely clicks for you. The first version of my statement looked something like this:

My true life's purpose is to use my creativity and drive to inspire and empower others, to live their highest purpose in life from a place of love, growth and purposeful action.

Do this next part of the exercise for a minimum of 30 minutes. Just start writing out that 'Life's Purpose' statement over and over, making subtle changes to it with each new version. What feels right? What do you want to change? What do you want to add? What do you want to take away?

The first time I ever did this, I literally wrote out the same statement for about 20 minutes, and nothing changed. But eventually it shifted, and then I had a breakthrough and the focus really started to come through. Most people don't realize that repetition calms the nervous system, allowing your logical "thinking" brain to let go a little. It lets you get to your deeper intuition (think of a monk repeating the same manta over and over again). At first there were little variations, then the variations got bigger, and then they came back around to what I was writing before. After about 90 minutes, I wrote something out that was so deeply profound to me that I almost started crying. I was holding back tears because, for the first time ever, I really felt that I had found my life's purpose. Try it today. It's okay if you don't hit on the exact statement the first time around — you can come back to it in 30 or 60 days after letting your subconscious have some time with it. It's a challenging exercise, but if you're willing to dedicate yourself to it, it can be incredibly profound. Here's what my statement looks like today:

I use my creativity and drive to inspire and empower others to live their highest purpose in life.

As you can see, this is what, not how: it's about the function, not the form. My function is to help others live their highest purpose. The form I use to do this varies depending on the context: I have High Impact Coaching, I have my TED Talk, I have this book, and my podcast: these are all forms of that same function of helping people live their highest purpose.

The Five Spokes of Life

When I was a kid I was a bit of a demon child. My parents got me a new bike for Christmas when I was 7 years old and apparently I took that as an invite to see how much punishment that bike could take.

I rode it down stairs, jumped it off dirt embankments, I even thought it was funny to ride it into chain link fences and bounce off. But I couldn't break that bike.

Until I got hit by a car. That did it (and did me in a bit too)

Don't worry. The car was only going about 15 miles per hour, but I was 7 and I still got scraped up pretty bad. But the worst part was that the car ran over the front wheel of the bike and ripped out about half the spokes. That was really what got me crying.

I tried riding the bike home, but without all the spokes, I couldn't get 10 feet without feeling like someone was hammering my 7-year old butt cheeks with a baseball bat.

Believe me, there is a reason for this story...

There are five key areas, or spokes, in each of our lives. These are, in no particular order:

1. Your career: your profession, or business
2. Your health: physical, mental, emotional, spiritual
3. Your finances: income, investments, monetary environment
4. Your relationships: intimate, friendship, family, others
5. Your contribution: how you are giving back to the community, and the world at large

A lot of people can spend a lot of energy and a lot of time on one or two of these areas but neglect the rest. It's kind of like trying to ride a bike that has only two spokes in its wheels — it's going to be a really bumpy ride for a really long time. We all know someone like this, right? Think of the executive who has only focused on his career and finances for the last 15 or 20 years. He might be successful in those parts of his life, but his relationships have gone to shit, he's got all sorts of health issues, and he's not contributing anything to society at all. That's not where we want to be.

We want to be rounded and growing in every area. Sure, there are going to be points in your life where you want to focus really intently on one spoke, but eventually, it's wise to come back and make sure that all five are getting the attention that they need. You'll rarely (if ever) have perfect equilibrium, but it's important to at least work towards your goals in all these areas over the long term.

So let's figure out what you want each of those five spokes to look like in your life. Grab your notebook and list out a minimum of three to five concrete details about what would be ideal in each of those five areas. Not what they might look like a year from now, or five years from now, but what they would look like if everything was ideal right now. It's fine if you have more bullet points — I've seen some people list as many as seven or ten — but at least put down a few very specific ideas about what 'ideal' looks like for you.

What do you want your career to look like? When I first did this, I wrote down that I wanted to be the leader of an organization of 100 people. I've always viewed myself as a leader, but I don't want to be the head of a big company of 50,000 people. I want to be the leader of a tight-knit family of 100 people that just creates a massive impact. I want to be working on something that's aligned with my joy. I want to be constantly learning in my career, every single day. I also want to have the freedom and flexibility to set my own schedule.

What do you want your financial situation to look like? Maybe you're earning $200,000 a year and you've got a million dollars in the bank. You've got another million dollars in investments that are incurring a minimum of 7% year over year growth. You own your home outright and have a year's worth of emergency expenses saved up in cash. Remember — this is about dreaming a little bit. Don't worry if you don't know how these details will actually become real. Just think about what's ideal. I redid my financial bullets recently because I'd made so much progress since I first did this exercise. When you start letting yourself dream, it's crazy what becomes possible.

What's ideal for your health? I want to be a particular weight with a particular amount of body fat. I want to eat a 90% plant-based diet, without being afraid to eat a burger or steak on the weekend. I want to feel strong and mobile, and to feel stronger and more mobile every year that I get older.

What are your ideal relationships? The first time I did the

Five Spokes exercises, I wrote down that I wanted to find an amazing and inspiring wife, along with all the details of what I was looking for in a wife. One of the reasons that Maddy and I are now married is because I had a list of 12 characteristics of something I wanted in a spouse, and Maddy matched 11 of them. Maddy had a four-page list (!), and I matched every point but one. We were both crystal clear on what was ideal for us, and so even though she was in Australia, and I was in the US, it was inevitable that we would figure it out. We were so clear on what we wanted in a partner that even though we were surrounded by millions of people closer to us, we went after the person 9000 miles away because they matched our list almost perfectly. Of course, it's not just your romantic relationship: what do you want your relationship with your kids and your friends and your siblings and parents and coworkers to look like? How much time are you spending with your family? How much time are you spending with your friends? Do you do monthly networking? Do you call your mom once a week?

Finally, what do you want your contribution to the world to look like? Maddy and I have made one of our biggest goals to have a massive contribution around the environment. Our goal is to plant 100,000 trees to help reverse the effect of carbon emissions. I also want to help 50,000 kids get an education that they wouldn't have otherwise been able to access. And then on an even bigger scale, I want to help 1% of the world live more from a place of purpose rather than a place of fear. Because I think if I can help 1% of the world do that, everybody else will solve all the other problems.

5 SPOKES

FINANCES

1. I am making $200K/year
2. I have $500K in investments growing at 15%
3.
4.
5.

CAREER

1. I own my own business and have a team of 5–10
2. I wake up Monday mornings feeling fulfilled and alive
3.
4.
5.

RELATIONSHIPS

1. I am happily married and spend weekly date nights with my partner
2. I have a strong relationship with my kids and never miss an event
3.
4.
5.

Goldilocks Goals and Affirmations

Now that we've gotten a little clarity on our direction, we need to do something with it... it's time to set some goals.

You may have heard something about how written-down goals are 50% more likely to be accomplished. But most of us don't know how to set goals in a way that actually leads us to accomplishing them. If you have no goals, your odds of success are pretty minimal — you're not aiming at anything!

A Yale study found that 97% of people never clarify their goals at all. But if you're in the 3% that does clarify their goals, the next step is to document them. Inc. found that the simple act of writing your goals down increases your chance of achieving them by 42%, which is massive. And then you want to share your goals and get accountability on them — the American Society of Training and Development found that this increased goal completion from 65% to 95% (and we're going to talk about accountability a whole lot more later on).

But it's not enough just to set a goal. We've all heard people say things like "Set bigger goals! It takes just as much energy to dream big as it does to dream small!" Well... maybe. The problem with setting really big goals is that you get discouraged when you don't see good progress. OK, so maybe we should set more achievable goals! Well... maybe. If your goals are too small then you're not going to be inspired or motivated to work towards them. I'd rather have a goal of making $100,000 and missing — but making, say, $90,000 — than having a goal of $10,000 and hitting it without any real effort.

So what's the right way to set a goal? A goal has two purposes:

- Clarity of direction
- Motivation to take action in the current moment.

The purpose of a goal is to get you to move your ass! If a goal does not accomplish the task of getting you into action, sometimes uncomfortable action, it is not doing its job.

That means you want a Goldilocks goal. You don't want it to be so big that it scares you off taking action, but not so small that it doesn't motivate you. You want your goal to be juuuust right. Many coaches suggest setting SMART goals, but I've found it's better to set SMMT goals (even if it doesn't sound as cool). Here's how:

1. Specific: saying "I want to make $100,000" rather than "I want to make more money"
2. Measurable: there should be a way you can objectively measure your success
3. Motivating: it has to drive you into action
4. Timebound: it has to have a deadline. Goals without deadlines are just dreams.

We talked earlier in the book about how affirmations and visualisations can help reprogram our subconscious mind, and now we're going to put our reticular activating system to work here to create affirmations around your Goldilocks Goals. Affirmations are intended to program our mind to interpret what we're saying as our current reality, and again, there are four components:

1. Make it personal: "I am..."
2. Use powerful feelings: "happy and grateful", "passionate and bold" (remember we need repetition and we need to evoke emotion)
3. Use the present tense: "now", "today" (this creates cognitive dissonance, which triggers your brain getting to work to create consistency between what you're saying and experiencing)
4. Use descriptive action words and adverbs: "proudly celebrating", "excitedly receiving", "passionately earning" (this creates a strong image for your subconscious to latch onto).

So — let's put that all together: "I am happy and grateful that I am now proudly celebrating my successful TED talk over drinks with friends and family" or "I am so happy and grateful that I am now passionately earning $25,000 per month through my online coaching business, serving others at the highest level". You want to be able to viscerally feel each of those experiences when you say your affirmation.

Now that we know how to put together Goldilocks Goals and Affirmations, let's start the process, right now. We're going to call this your Next Level Goal.

Next Level Goal Setting Exercise

Every year or so, I set ONE major goal, that is an absolutely game changer for my life. And I call it my Next Level Goal.

When you achieve your Next Level Goal, everything will be different. You'll be a different person entirely! You've gone up a level in your life, and you can never go back down. This goal should be able to be accomplished in 12 to 18 months, it should stretch you out of your comfort zone — but not so much that it makes you freeze — and finally, you shouldn't be able to see a clear path to accomplishing it right now. This is a big challenge for a lot of people, but remember, the purpose of a goal is to get you to take action now and if you already knew how to achieve this goal, you would have already done it. Don't worry — as you start to take action, you're going to uncover the path.

Here are some examples of a Next Level Goal:

- Bestselling book
- TED Talk
- $25k per month (or even $100k per month!)
- Good Morning America interview
- iTunes Top 25 podcast
- Quit your day job to run your six-figure consulting business

Take a few minutes to think about this, and then write down three of these Next Level Goals that feel right and exciting to you, based on everything you've learned so far in this section on Clarity.

Then, on a scale of 1 to 10, compare how each of the three goals align with your...

- Life purpose
- 3 to 5 joy paradigms
- 5 spokes vision

Do this for each of the goals you laid out. Then you want to pick one (maybe two) that scores highest out of a possible score of 30. This should be the goal that scores highest on allowing you to live your life's purpose, to stay in your joy paradigms, and to achieve as much of your 5 spokes vision as possible.

Once you've done this exercise and settled on the Next Level Goal that's right for you, make yourself a note: focus is a limited resource. You can't achieve five or six big goals like this in one year. Your focus is like a battery — you only have so much attention and energy that you can put out before you run dry. This is what I call the Focus Law of Squares, and we'll talk more about that in Chapter 9.

Now it's time to create the affirmation to go with this goal, just like we outlined before. Make it personal, use powerful feelings, use the present tense, and use descriptive action words to really bring it to life. We're going to make a movie out of it:

- Write it down and then read it ten times. Each time you read it, put a little more energy into it — really viscerally *feel* it. Recite it in your head like you were about to go on stage in the theater.

- Close your eyes and repeat it one more time. "I am so happy and grateful that now..." and actually imagine what life is like now that you've accomplished this goal. Notice where you are, what's going on, who's there with you. How does it feel in your body?
- Allow that feeling to swell and spread all through your body, and when it feels complete, take a big, deep breath. Open your eyes and come back.

You just made a movie! That's what we call a visualization. Do this affirmation and visualization every day for 30 days. Focus on feeling it, really sensing everything that's happening in your life because you've achieved this goal.

Remember that your subconscious responds to repetition and emotion, so make sure you take a minute to separate yourself from your daily life so that you can get really immersed in it. This is how I achieved my first Next Level Goal of getting on stage with Jack Canfield and telling everyone how I just made over $100k/mo in my coaching business less than a year after starting.

And don't be surprised if you feel a little bit stressed after doing this for a while: you're intentionally creating cognitive dissonance, which is your brain's discomfort with the gap between where you are currently and what you're visualizing. That's okay! That's actually what we're aiming for, because that discomfort is what creates action.

Now, We're creating so much clarity around where you actually need to be, that it's like drawing back a really strong bow, and aiming you — the arrow — at your target. It's strenuous. It's stressful. When you create this much clarity, it's both scary and extremely motivating. Often coaching clients will get on a call after going through these exercises and say things like, "Zander, I'm freaking out. I've got to quit my job this week. I have to get moving right now." If that's you after these exercises, that's awesome. But pump the brakes and hold steady for a second. Getting you to this stage was intentional, but you've got a few more things to pin down.

SIX

LOVE WHAT YOU DO

"Discovering your purpose is the most significant thing you will do in your life, and you, your loved ones, and the world will be better off because you went on this journey."

MASTIN KIPP

In the last chapter we went through a lot of exercises to help you figure out what you want and love. That's the first part of the Clarity equation. Sadly, it's just not enough to love the work you do — you also have to be good at it, and it's got to be something that people want and will pay for.

It seems obvious that you have to be good at the thing you're going to work on, right? But I'm not just talking about being competent at something. Being competent is the bare minimum. What I'm talking about here is being *good* at something — like, really good. The significantly-better-than-other-people kind of good.

And while we are focusing here on what you can do with your career or business, your high-level skills might not be related to what you're getting paid for right now. That's fine. We're going to work through some questions and see if there might be some overlap.

Discover Your Gifts

Step One: Ask yourself these primer questions:

- What do your friends say you're great at? (If you don't know what it is, ask your friends.)
- What do you see other people struggling with? (Often if you notice other people struggling with something, it's because it comes more easily to you.)

Step Two: List out 5 gifts you have in each of the following categories:

- Skills that you've developed over the years
- For example: personal communication, sales, juggling
- Knowledge that you've built up
- For example: real estate investment, fitness/nutrition/wellness, tech/programming
- Obstacles you've overcome
- For example: divorce, being broke, physical trauma
- Accomplishments you may have had
- For example: top salesperson, SAT score, Masters degree, bodybuilding champ, getting a raise/promotion

Step Three: Mark each 'gift' as either high value or low value (+/-) to others.

(Would people pay for help with it? By the end of this you should end up with an idea of what gifts you have that are of high social value to other people.)

- Overcoming heartbreak (+)
- Juggling (-)
- Helping a business 10X their income (+)
- Excel spreadsheet expertise (- - - -) (just kidding. Some people love spreadsheets)

Step Four: Review your notes and pick an area to brainstorm and pursue further:

- Pick a topic that can incorporate several of your gifts (the more high value the better), while doing something you LOVE
- The thing you focus on should light you up just to think about it
- Remember: this won't be the last thing you ever do, but you have to start somewhere. Starting here will help you work your way forward into something that's an even better fit.

Appreciating Your Own Gifts

This exercise is exciting, right? It starts to show you all the things that you're already really good at, and where you already have the capabilities that people would pay for. But when you're trying to look at yourself, it can be hard to appreciate what you're really great at. Other people, looking at you from the outside, can immediately see what you're great at and point out every one of your skills. But you can't read the label from inside the bottle. You only know your own experiences, and you don't have any frame of reference for how you stack up among all the people doing what you're doing. You don't know any better, and so you don't realise quite how good you actually are. Nearly 100% of the people I've ever worked with have undervalued their own gifts and abilities, simply because they don't know any better, and that can kill your business before it ever gets off the ground.

Let me show you what I mean.

We work a lot with health and wellness practitioners who are coming into the coaching space. So *many* of them have this completely messed-up mindset around what they can and can't charge people in order to help them.

We had a health and nutrition coach that was stellar at what she did. We will call her Lindsey (because that was her name). Lindsey had experience as a coach and a degree as a Registered Dietitian. But she was working three part-time jobs just to pay the bills because even though she was working forty hours a week in her business, she was barely making coffee money. She had undervalued herself. After months of doing this, she was exhausted and she wanted to quit.

Luckily, she started working with us and we helped her understand what her skills were really worth, so she could start to command her true value (and make the money she deserved). After a couple months she was able to start charging prices like $3000 for her services and quit all of her part-time jobs. Now she makes multiple six figures every year in her business and employs other R.D.s underneath her.

This is why you *must* understand the true value of your gifts. If you don't recognise that value, your clients won't either.

Let's say you're a health coach and you specialize in helping people lose weight sustainably. What's that actually worth to somebody? Well, you might say, a gym membership is $20 a month. Jenny Craig is $30 per month. But is having a gym membership or a Jenny Craig plan the same thing as getting results? Is it sustainable and healthy? Will it help keep the weight off? No. Most people have already tried those options and they have failed. It doesn't matter how much those options cost: they didn't have the right knowledge, action plan, troubleshooting and accountability to get where they wanted to be.

So what would it actually be worth for somebody who's 50 pounds overweight, to finally lose the 50 pounds and keep it off for the rest of their life? To have the energy to be there for their kids, to reignite the spark in their marriage, to have the confidence to show up at a higher level at work, to not die from a chronic illness at an early age? What is that actually worth to someone? It's worth far, far more than any gym membership, and if those outcomes are what you can help them create, they will happily pay you far more too.

And that's not even taking into account how long you've spent becoming an expert in your space. How many months or years have you spent? How much money? What's one year of your time and education worth? Think about it: if it took you a decade and $20,000 to learn everything you know now, wouldn't it be worth it to your customers to pay you not to have to go through that themselves? Not only are you helping people with the thing they most need help with, but you're saving people time — the one resource we can never get back. That's invaluable.

The Curse of Knowledge

It's really hard to put yourself in somebody else's shoes and truly understand what it is that they want and what it is that they need. This is called the curse of knowledge, which is also one of the reasons why we undervalue ourselves. Once we've gained some knowledge — once we've learned something new, or gotten good at a skill — we tend to assume that everybody else also has the same knowledge or ability that we do. We forget what it's like to *not* have that knowledge.

There's a story in *Made to Stick* called "Tappers and Listeners". The authors put 120 people into a room and gave them a list of songs that everybody would know, like 'Twinkle, Twinkle, Little Star', 'Happy Birthday', 'Jingle Bells', and so on. They put everyone into pairs: one tapper, one listener. They told the tapper the name of the song and the tapper had to tap out the tune on the table, so that the listener could guess which one it was. Later they polled each tapper about how they expected the listeners to do, and most tappers said they thought the listeners would get about 50% of the songs right. In fact, the listeners only got 2.5% of the songs right. The tappers couldn't imagine what the listener was experiencing, without that extra little bit of knowledge about which song it was.

It makes sense, right? If you were to tap out 'Twinkle Twinkle Little Star', you would hear that song playing in your head, but the listener would just be hearing you tapping away randomly on the table. We run into a lot of problems when we think everybody else knows what we know. The reality is that they don't. Your future customers don't know what you know, they don't have the experience you have, and they *really* want access to what you have.

The second part of the curse of knowledge is that knowing something doesn't necessarily make you good at communicating about what you know. This is the reason I was one of the highest- paid engineers at my seniority level at Cisco: I didn't need a salesperson. All the other engineers did, because they couldn't effectively communicate what they were doing to clients. But I could: I had the ability to communicate really complex technologies in very simple ways that business leaders could understand and run the deal on my own. I ended up making about 30% more than all the other engineers of my experience level, because I knew how to communicate my value. They had all the same training, all the same tools and resources — but they couldn't help other people to understand what they knew. I had a quota of $130 million and I ran much of it on my own without a salesperson. I would get raises and promotions when they wouldn't, and it was because I could communicate my value.

Communicating Your Value

Two salesmen walk into the manager's office.

He's only going to be hiring one for the new highly paid role to lead his sales team, so he puts his prized MontBlanc pen down on the desk and tells the candidates, "Sell me this pen."

The first man picks up the pen and starts detailing the top features and benefits of the beautifully crafted pen:

- Perfectly weighted and balanced
- The smoothest ink flow on the market
- Solid gold accents and platinum coated handle
- One of a kind engraving

The manager shrugs. "Meh."

The second man picks up the pen and asks the manager "one of us is getting the sales lead today right?"

"Yep, only one."

"And you will need to sign the contract today, right?"

"Yep, right after this meeting"

"Do you have another pen?"

"Actually, no I do not."
"I'll sell you this one for a dollar."
"The job is yours."

Learning to communicate your value definitely requires confidence. It also takes practice. But it's mostly about learning how to understand what people really want and need. Instead of saying, "My service is worth X", it's about asking, "What would it be worth to solve this problem for you?" and then helping them see that your service is the exact solution they need to solve the problem.

Did you notice what happened there? It stopped being about you and the service or product (in this case, the pen) that you can provide. It became about them, and the problem they want and need solved. Up until this point we've been very focused on you: what you want, what you love, what you're good at. But all of that is in service of something much greater than you. This can be kind of a gut punch to a lot of people after doing all this self-development work. You get so much clarity about what really matters to you, you suddenly understand your purpose, you know what you want to do in life... and then along comes Zander to burst your bubble. Sorry, buddy. But the world is not about you. It is important for you to understand what is important for you. But now you have to take that and align it to the world outside.

I believe that when you're aligned with your true self, and with the universe, that's when you're the most fulfilled, that's when the most success will come to you. It's a combination of these two things. If you're just in it for you, you have the wrong energy and intention. When you start to understand it's about taking what makes you, you, and what you're good at, what you love and what drives you *and* then finding a way to connect it to what the external world needs, that's when you start to see success.

Years ago I had a conversation with Adam Toren, who is the co-founder of *Entrepreneur*. We were chatting about helping new coaches get their businesses up and running. And he goes, "Oh, dude, congrats, props to you. I could never do that." This guy is crazy successful, so I was kinda surprised, and asked him why. He said, "To be honest, new coaches are selfish." *What?* I was shocked. All the people we work with are coming from a place of service. They want to help people. How could that be selfish? He said, "If somebody is not making at least six figures in their business, or in their career, it's because they're selfish". *Dude, not helping.* I had to ask him again to expand on what he meant.

Adam went on to explain that the reason most early-stage coaches are not making the money that they need to make is because they're so focused on little things that don't matter. They're so obsessed with getting their logo right that they forget about getting their gifts out to the world. They put off releasing their program for months or years until every last tiny detail is perfect, and meanwhile their potential customers are crying themselves to sleep at night because their problem is so painful. The coach is too afraid to put themselves out there and possibly be rejected — to actually go find those people, and enroll them, and make money, and go help them change their life — and that's about as selfish as it gets. They have all the gifts, and they're not sharing them, because they're too afraid of someone saying no. Their fears are more important to them than actually getting out there and helping people.

Well, damn.

That lit a fire under my ass, and it's become something I make a point of talking about. Every time I post about it on social media I get two types of comments: the first type is, "This is the best post that I've ever seen, this is totally me." The second is, "You're a dick, go to hell". It's a polarizing position, and I get that, but it's true: fear is a self-centered emotion and mindset. It's inherently selfish. There's a place for fear, like we talked about at the start, but not here. Not when it's stopping you from sharing your gifts, not when it's stopping you from changing people's lives. And now that you know that, it's time to get moving.

A QUICK ASK FROM THE AUTHOR...

My goal is to get *Sh*t You Don't Learn In College* to as many people that need it as possible.

So if you have gotten anything valuable from this text so far, please leave us a review wherever you got this book (Amazon, Audible, Facebook, etc) to let people know how much it's helped you.

It'll only take 60 seconds and your review might change someone's life. Thank you, and let's get back to it.

EXECUTION

"Zander, what's more important for me to be successful? Is it my mindset, my skill set, or my toolset?" asked Griffin, a student and good friend of mine.

"Let me ask you this. How long could you balance on a stool with only one or two legs?" I responded.

"Uhhh...stupid question."

"I agree. Honestly, with the right mindset you can always build the right skillset and the right toolset. But without all three you're not gonna stay up for very long."

Up to this point in the book we have focussed pretty heavily on what I call "Prep work" — understanding how our brain works, getting clarity, how to change your programming, etc. But that's only half of the equation.

To understand the second half (and what will become the focus for the later part of this book) we need to understand what I call the Success Hierarchy and start executing toward our goals.

The Success Hierarchy

The Success Hierarchy is a pyramid with five layers. Each of these layers represents something you need to be successful, and every single one needs to be in place for you to really achieve the success you want.

SUCCESS HIERARCHY

At the top of the pyramid we have tools. Let's say you're in a sales role — what are the tools you need to be successful? You need a phone so you can call people. You need a laptop, an email application, and a calendar application. Now 'tools' might be the smallest piece at the very top, because tools are generally easy to learn. But could you imagine trying to be a successful sales person without a phone or a laptop? Just because they are easier to learn doesn't make them less necessary for success.

Underneath that you have the skills that help you be successful. As a salesperson, you have communication skills, rapport-building skills, objection-handling skills, deal-closing skills.

Then underneath that, you have systems. Let's say you work for a solar company. Your solar company gives you a specific process to use when you are reaching out to people, and a specific process for how to open up conversations and walk through the sales process. Now, this is where a lot of people stop when it comes to the success hierarchy. These initial three layers are all very tangible elements that you need to be successful. But it's the final two layers that really make all the difference.

The next piece is your mindset. Let's take John A and John B. Let's say John A and John B are both in a sales role at the solar company. John A has the exact same tools, skills and systems as John B. John A is confident. He's an action taker. He's certain, he's decisive, he moves forward with things and he's not afraid of setbacks. John B, on the other hand, is indecisive and hesitant. He doesn't make decisions quickly and he's scared of taking action. Which John is going to be successful? John A, the one who's got the right mindset, the right beliefs, the right confidence. It sounds obvious, but a lot of people miss this. And this is why we've spent so much time focusing on helping you learn how to reprogram your brain and have different beliefs.

Finally, there's your energy and intention. One of the things I've noticed since starting my business is that people are done with the bullshit. People are done with being manipulated. Your future customers don't want to deal with people who are trying to take advantage. And so the people that are going to be the most successful moving forward are the people that are doing things for the right reason, the people that are putting out good energy. If you're here to serve, if you're here to help, if you're coming from a good place where your intention is to help make a better world? Then you're exactly the kind of person that people want to do business with.

Have you ever seen the movie *Matilda*? If you didn't (you should), Matilda is a little girl with telekinetic powers. Her parents are horrible people, and her dad especially. He's a used car salesman, played by Danny DeVito, and he spends the whole movie trying to sell dodgy, dangerous cars to people who don't know any better. That's the image that a lot of people have in mind when it comes to dealing with salespeople (and if you're going to be an entrepreneur, you're also going to be a salesperson). We don't want even a hint of that negative manipulative energy near your business. You want people to think of you as a trusted advisor, someone who has peoples' best interests at heart, who understands and supports and loves their customers. I think of Yoda, from *Star Wars*. Now, Yoda is not always going to tell you what you want to hear. But Yoda is going to tell you what you need to hear, and he has your best interest in mind. And because of that, you trust Yoda more than you trust yourself.

Like I said before, you need all of these things to be successful. Having good intentions and a strong mindset are key, but they won't do much for you if you don't have the system, skills and tools. And you could have the best tools, skills and systems in the world, but you're always going to be fighting an uphill battle if you don't have the right energy, intention and mindset. So let's make sure you are building all five moving forward.

SEVEN

GROWTH SUCKS

"So what do we do? Anything. Something. So long as we just don't sit there. If we screw it up, start over. Try something else. If we wait until we've satisfied all the uncertainties, it may be too late."

LEE IACOCCA

When you're in college (or any other period of your life, for that matter) nobody teaches you how to execute. Or, in other words, how to get shit done.

One of the first pieces of business advice I ever got was, "Find a mentor. Learn from someone that has been where you are and gotten to where you want to be. Everyone else's advice is just 'best guess B.S.'"

So if you want to be a college professor I guess it makes sense to learn the skills they teach you in college right? But what if you want to do something else? What if you want to be an entrepreneur? Or a philanthropist? Or a professional sports player?

When you're in school no one teaches how to execute and be successful from practical experience. Or in other words, how to get shit done in the REAL world.

Remember the two johns from earlier? You can have all the tools and the tactics, but if you never learn what it really takes to execute, you're going to struggle. Knowing how to get the job done is the difference between a $50,000 income and a $200,000 income — or more. The tools and tactics are not what matter; it's your mindset, the way you work and how you learn.

Now, you might think, "Zander, I hauled ass all through college. I show up to work every day and get stuff done. What do you mean I don't know how to do this?"

Do you really think success in school translates to success in life?

Maybe for some. But execution at college or in a day job is fundamentally different to execution in your own business — in fact it might even detract from your ability to succeed! According to one study[1], 77% of the sample group of self-made millionaires were not A-students. Most of them got Bs and Cs all the way through school and college, and when it came time to start their businesses, they had a huge advantage. Unlike the A-students, they had a wider range of interests, and so they found it easier to discover work that really lit them up (they had an easier time getting clarity on their direction). They were more risk-tolerant, and focused on growth rather than appearances, and so they were rewarded more often. And finally, they were less prone to anxiety. They already knew how not to sweat the small stuff. Being successful in college and the traditional professional world is about being good at the one moment when it counts — rocking the exam or presentation or event. In both environments, you only get one shot, and if you make a mistake, it's rare that you get any kind of do-over.

But outside those high-pressure bubbles, it doesn't work that way. Entrepreneurship is about speed of execution, not perfection of preparation. To get this you need to understand the Engineering Agile Model — let's get nerdy for a minute! In engineering there's a concept called the minimum viable product. This is the most basic, rudimentary, C-grade version of your offering that you can come up with. It is not even close to perfect, and the point of the minimum viable product is that by putting something out quickly, you get feedback. Your work comes into contact with the real world quickly, and so you can refine it, make it better, and iterate towards perfection. This is so crucial. If you come at your work with an A-student mentality — that everything has to be perfect first time around — you will spend far too long fiddling with something that the market might not want at all. You can work for months or even years in a vacuum, without feedback, and discover much too late that what you're trying to sell doesn't appeal to anyone. So you purposefully put out C-grade work to learn from the market, to figure out what people want and like and will pay for, so that you can refine your offer and make it better, until eventually, you've refined it so much that you end up with an A+ product. This is not taught in school. We're not taught to fail. We're not taught to seek out real-world feedback. We are not taught to collaborate with others (collaborating in high school is called "cheating" in case you were wondering; learned that the hard way.) And that is a crime, because these are fundamental skills. Iteration and repetition and feedback create mastery.

The Growth Cycle

When I was first starting my business I remember my mom called me one day and asked me.

"Zander, what do you do every day?"

"Well Mama," (yes I call my mom mama) "Every morning I wake up. I try something new. I screw it up, and I learn from my mistakes so I can do it better tomorrow."

That may have been the wisest thing to ever come out of my mouth.

In order for you to get something you currently don't have, you have to become someone that you currently are not. In order to become that person, you have to grow. Whether it's personally, in your relationships, in your business skills, wherever it might be, you have to grow.

The four steps to growth are pretty straightforward, but implementing them is another story and that's why this chapter is so important. If you are implementing this cycle properly, it's gonna suck.

First, we need direction and a plan (which we accomplished in the clarity section). Then, we need to take action (which can be scary if you don't feel like you know what you are doing or your plan is faulty). Then, we need to reflect on the actions we took (also scary when most of the time, your actions lead to some form of failure or not accomplishing your goal), and lastly we need a to correct the initial plan and direction, so that you can iterate closer to where you want to go.

This is the Growth Cycle, and each time you come to the end of the cycle, you go back to the beginning. Ray Dalio, one of the greatest investors in the world, calls this the virtuous cycle.

THE GROWTH CYCLE

So we've already got direction nailed down (and if you don't, go back to the Clarity section and work through the exercises there until you do). Direction is the fundamental first step in this cycle: you need to have some idea of what you're working towards before anything else can happen, even if it's only 30% of the jigsaw puzzle right now. Then there's action, and this is fairly intuitive for most of us, though not for all. Once we have direction, we can start to figure out what we would need to do to end up at our goal. Now, while any action is better than nothing (what we call imperfect action) we normally want to make sure we are at least pointed in the right direction before we start sprinting headstrong in the wrong direction. So here's a little guide to make sure you at least have a "recipe" to bake your cake with before you try and bake one all by yourself without one (trust me, no one wins when you do that):

- Where do you want to end up?
- Who do you know that has accomplished something similar and could teach you about what actions to take? (Normally the first step in acting is to get clear mentorship and support)
- If you don't know anyone, who do you know that might know someone and could introduce you?
- If that still doesn't work, what resources can you find to point you in the right direction? Google? YouTube? Blogs? Podcasts? Books? Facebook groups? It's the information age! We have all the answers at our fingertips.

Unlike action, the next part is really not intuitive for most of us. Reflection is hard, because most of the time we're head-down, working away, and to stop and review what has and hasn't been effective seems like an annoying waste of time. Let's say you want to hit six figures in your business this year as an entrepreneur. Well, how many days of the year do you actually accomplish that goal? If you hit that goal, you hit it on a single day. One day you have not made six figures, and the next day you have. But that "one day" is the result of what you've been doing for all the other days. Now, if you do hit the six-figure goal, then reflection is going to feel good. Even if some things didn't work, there's obviously enough that did work for you to reach that milestone.

But if you don't hit the goal, reflection is going to feel scary and depressing. I get it: reflecting on what's not working isn't fun. It's like turning on lights in a big dark room. You don't want to see what's in there. You don't want to admit that you failed. You don't want to admit that something messed up. But at the root of this fear is the fixed mindset. It's the belief that if you did something wrong, you're a failure and you're always going to be a failure. It's the belief that if you're a failure, everyone will judge you, or that you're never going to be able to make this thing work. This is why you've gotta root out the fixed mindset, because none of that is true. If you didn't hit your goal, it just means that the actions you took didn't have the outcome you wanted. It's an experiment, and you learned something. It might be a painful experiment — you might realise that you're not actually doing all the stuff you thought you were. You might find that you're not as productive as you thought you were, or that you've been avoiding doing something that could make a big difference. And there's no denying that those realizations suck. But you've got to be able to reflect on which particular actions didn't work, so that you can move on to correction.

Correction is how you break through to the next level, and actually move yourself closer to where you want to be. This is where you actively look at what you can do differently: "if that didn't work, what will? What's my next experiment, and how will I know if it works?" Correction is the exciting bit. This is where entrepreneurship gets creative and how you get to put your stamp on things — the solutions you come up with during the correction phase of this cycle are going to be unique to you, they're going to give you an edge, and they're going to hone your direction even more, so that the virtuous cycle can begin again.

Knowledge Is Not Power

This is a shocking idea for many people. But knowledge isn't power. If it were, all the universities in the world would be the most powerful institutions in the world. Are they? No, they're not. They have some power, for sure, but not enough to change the world. And in my opinion, knowledge for knowledge's sake is actually the mortal enemy of wisdom. Because we can get into a cycle of learning as a form of procrastination, rather than implementing that knowledge through action, and thus creating wisdom.

And more than just procrastination, learning stuff just for the sake of learning stuff looks suspiciously like an addiction. Just like when you get a hit of your substance of choice, you get a hit when you learn something new. You read a book, you learn something, and you get a dopamine response from learning it. But what happens when you go to turn that knowledge into wisdom? You face challenges, you face trials, you face tribulations. So rather than facing them and taking action, and moving forward, you go learn something else in search of another dopamine hit. It's a downward spiral.

The only way is to persist with implementing the knowledge you learn, so that it becomes wisdom. It's about taking your curiosity and turning it into something tangible, using what you learn to solve actual problems — not using the learning itself as a way to avoid those problems.

This is something that I'm incredibly passionate about when it comes to success. In the early stages of writing this book, I recorded 15 episodes of my podcast, also called Shit You Don't Learn in College. In each episode I interview another successful entrepreneur, and one of the questions I ask now is "What is the biggest mistake you made in college, or the one thing you wish you'd learned in college but didn't?" 10 of my 15 guests said that they spent too much time learning and not enough time implementing. I think that might be the biggest mistake that people make.I'm not saying you shouldn't try to learn stuff or that you should never read anything again. You definitely should — most CEOs and successful people are readers. But they're readers who implement. They read with a purpose. They read to figure out how to solve problems and expand their thinking, so that they can go take more effective action.

The point of this book is to help you create a life with more money, more meaning and more freedom. And if you get addicted to learning, and you never put that knowledge into action, it will prevent you from doing the things that will get you more money, more meaning and more freedom.

Success Loves Speed

Let's look at growth as a graph. You're starting from the bottom left corner in the graph, and your goal is in the top right corner. Between you and your goal lies growth. We know now that growth is an iterative process. We have to go through these iterative loops of creating direction, taking some action, failing a bunch, reviewing the action, adjusting the direction, adjusting the action and so on.

SUCCESS LOVES SPEED

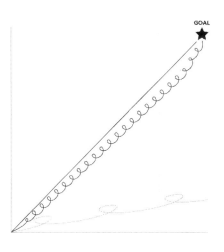

Most of us go through this process really, really slowly. We want to be safe and careful (which, you'll remember, is what we were taught in school — go slowly and get it perfect). So you end up with a trajectory like the green loops: slow and steady. You might go through the cycle every few months, whenever you make an adjustment in your life. You can get to your goal that way — it's just going to take you a really, really long time. But if you speed up that iterative process, you condense the learning to a much shorter period of time, and you start to take action faster, fail faster, learn faster and progress faster, so it starts to look more like the blue loops. The faster you can act and adjust, act and adjust, the faster you're going to get to your goal. Ray Dalio talks about this in his book, *Principles*. Just realize that the longer you stretch out this cycle, the longer it's going to take you to reach that goal. The only thing that makes us stretch this out is fear. Fear of messing up, fear of imperfection, fear of judgement or criticism — and none of that fear is worth it. When you feel yourself delaying the next stage in the cycle, go to your fear journal. Hash it out. And then get to work, and go fast.

Go For No

If you wanted to publish a book, how many times would you have to hear 'no' from publishers before you gave up? 10? 20? 30?

Jack Canfield was denied by 144 publishers for the idea of *Chicken Soup For The Soul*, before it finally got picked up.

500,000,000 books later, *Chicken Soup* is one of the top selling books of all time! Could you imagine if he stopped after 30 rejections?

In the book *Go For No*, the authors talk about one of the biggest differentiators between successful and unsuccessful people.Richard Fenton and Andrea Waltz explain that your success depends on your relationship with failure and rejection:

- The first level of success is simply having the ability to fail — and this is everybody. Everybody can fail, 100% of the population.
- The second level of success is the willingness to fail. As you move to the willingness to fail, they say only about 20% of all people will make it to level two for any sustained period of time. So 80% of people never become willing to fail. The 20% who do become the world's more successful people.
- The third level is moving from willingness to fail to 'wantingness' to fail: you actually *want* to fail because you know that failure brings growth and brings success, and you want to condense that process. This will be about 5% of the population, which becomes the top 5% of society, about 1 in 20 people.
- Then you get to level four, which is where people are trying to fail bigger and faster, because they know that the faster you fail, the faster you grow, and faster you grow, the bigger that you grow. So not only do they want to do it, they want to do it bigger than other people and faster than other people. This is the top 1%. They'll make it to professional sports, become political influencers, or become multi-millionaires.
- The last level is "failing exponentially", which means helping others fail forward in the same way you did. This is where you see the Steve Jobs, Elon Musk, Jeff Bezos types of the world. Not only are

they not afraid to fail and iterate, and want to do it bigger and faster than everybody, but they create an entire culture and an entire society of people that want to do the same thing. This is the top .001% of people that create that culture and society of willingness to grow and fail amongst everybody else.

All this to say; if you want to have a huge impact, if you want the extra money, meaning and freedom, focus on failing. Don't be afraid of it. It's the way forward.

Legendary ice hockey coach Wayne Gretzky said that you will miss 100% of the shots you don't take. If you never ask for something, if you never take a risk, it's the only way you are guaranteed to fail. Whether that's in your relationship, whether that's in your business, whether that's in your career, personal life, doesn't matter. The only way to fail is not to try.

The $5 Challenge.

This is one of my favorite exercises. Go pull $20 out of the bank in one-dollar notes. Then you're going to go out in public and you're going to ask 20 different people for $5. You're not allowed to tell them why, you're not allowed to explain what you're doing. You just have to introduce yourself and ask them if you can have $5.

The big kicker is that if they give you $5, you're going to give them the $5 back and $1 extra. The whole goal here is to learn how to handle hearing "no". Because you're not allowed to explain why you're doing what you're doing, most people are going to say no to your request. But you know that you're going to be able to make somebody's day whenever you hear "yes", right? They're gonna get a little extra back when they agree to give you $5. Knowing that is going to help you make it through all the "no"s. And every time that you hear "no", you're going to learn that it doesn't kill you. And when you do finally hear yes, and you get to give that person back 6 bucks, and they get to be like, what the hell and you get to explain what it is. That's gonna make both of your days. This is not just about getting used to hearing "no", but learning to *want* to hear "no", so that eventually you can get to a yes and make somebody's day.

You have to let your enthusiasm come through in this one. You have to believe in what you're doing, because belief is contagious. This is not about playing a zero-sum game: someone else doesn't have to lose for you to win.

Lots of people believe that whenever they're selling something or taking money for a service, that it's a zero sum game — for me to make $5 this person has to lose $5. But it's not true at all. Let's say you bought an iPhone recently. How much did you pay for it? Probably around a thousand bucks, right? But when you bought that iPhone, were you like, "Damn you Apple, you stole my $1000!" No! I bet you thought, "Oh my God, I love this thing." Apple wins, you win, everybody wins, because you get something that is more than worth the money you spent and Apple gets cash in the bank. You get something that is actually worth more than $1000 to you, otherwise you would not have paid that much for it. So you receive something of greater value than $1000, and Apple receives a value of exactly $1000. So it's not a zero sum game: every time there's a trade like that, the value the buyer receives is *more* than what they spent. If you're in sales, or you run your own business, every time somebody pays you for something, you're gonna get to give them more in return. Whether it's a service, whether it's a product — if somebody buys my service for $6,000, they're gonna get $20,000 worth of value from it. So I have no problem asking them to pay the $6,000, because I know the value they're going to get from it is going to be absolutely transformational and of much higher value than the dollar amount.

---

1. https://www.forbes.com/sites/mikekappel/2019/07/15/sorry-overachievers-cs-are-all-you-need-in-business/

EIGHT

THE UNSTOPPABLE FORCE VS THE IMMOVABLE OBJECT

"The secret of getting things done is to act."

DANTE ALIGHIERI

If it hasn't already become obvious, a huge part of the Sh*t You Don't Learn In College is about how to start taking courageous action in the face of fear, judgement, and criticism in a way that will move you towards the life and career of your dreams. In this chapter, we're going to talk about becoming action oriented, so that you can get moving, and keep moving.

Get Moving, Stay Moving

Momentum is one of the most important forces in life, and its opposite, inertia, is one of the most dangerous. Inertia makes you an immovable object, but momentum makes you an unstoppable force. But moving from inertia to momentum is truly challenging. Think about a 30-car freight train. To get that thing moving, you need a hell of a lot of force. The engine is going full bore, the gears are pumping, and for quite a while you just hear this grinding, groaning sound. It's not going, it's not going, and then it starts to inch forward, so slowly, the wheels are slipping because it's so heavy and the inertia of it is so strong. But eventually it starts to move, and slowly it speeds up: 2 mph, 5 mph, 10 mph, 30 mph, 50 mph and then all of a sudden it's flying — and good luck getting it to stop.

In case it's not obvious, you're the train in this analogy. Getting moving is really hard. It's such a struggle that for most people, it's almost impossible to get going, because they push and push and push, and they get discouraged that it's taking so long to get going. But the moment you stop, even if it's just for a second, all the momentum that was starting to build just vanishes. You may have been inching forward but now you've gone straight back to frozen. So the most important thing, especially at the beginning, is not to stop. The hardest work always come upfront — if you can push through all the inertia and resistance, you'll suddenly find yourself flying along with incredible momentum.

The 5-Second Rule and The First Step

BEEP BEEP BEEP BEEP

It's four in the morning and I definitely don't want to get out of bed right now. I'm exhausted. Whose idea was this? Not a sane person, that's for sure.

But before I start to think too much and talk myself into hitting snooze, I hear a tiny voice in the back of my mind start counting down:

"5... 4... 3... 2...1." I sit straight up in bed with my eyes wide open. I'm awake.

Coach and bestselling author Mel Robbins has a very simple rule for helping you start to actually build some of that momentum — she calls it the 5-Second Rule.

It's pretty simple: when you have a moment of clarity, and you feel the need to take action, do it within five seconds, or your brain will kill that momentum. For example: if you're sitting on the couch watching Netflix and you have an inclination to go do some research on how to launch your business, if you don't do it within five seconds, that desire will be gone. As soon as you have the idea or the spark to go do something, count backwards from 5, and as soon as you get to 1, start moving. Otherwise your brain is going to cut in with all the reasons why you shouldn't do it, and the opportunity will be gone.

Like I said before, the hardest work comes at the beginning of the process. Making the decision to get up off the couch, where you're comfortable and relaxed, is the most difficult part of the entire process. Once you're up, it's easy to grab your laptop, open Google, and start searching. It's easy to start getting creative and following your instinct about what you need to figure out. It's just the choice to act that's difficult. This is where I always think of Martin Luther King's great quote: "You don't have to see the whole staircase, just take the first step." Once you take the first step, the second step is easier. The third step is easier. The fourth step is easier. The first step is difficult, but every step after that gets easier.

The reason the first step is so hard is that most of us are living pretty comfortable lives already. We've put down roots, we've settled in, even if it's not the life that we really wanted. Those roots make it really difficult for you to move forward, and believe me, I can relate. I was incredibly comfortable in my nine to five, making over $200,000 per year. And I was on the path to become even more comfortable. Had I been offered a managerial role at Cisco, I would probably still be there, because it would have been just enough extra comfort to keep me. But this is how it happens — how we get stuck and rooted down in a life we don't really want. Maybe we make a bit more money, we get a little bit more vacation time, we get a little more responsibility. But we also have a big mortgage. The nice car lease, the private school tuition for the kids. Now that comfort looks a lot more like a jail cell. Because comfort is not the same as happiness. The golden handcuffs get bigger. Just because something feels comfortable and familiar doesn't mean it's right for you. It's just easy because it's what you know. And so now we've gotta get comfortable with what we don't know.

The Colin Powell Rule

During the Bush administration, including the 9/11 attacks, and the US's subsequent war on terror, Colin Powell was the Secretary of State. He was responsible for making incredibly stressful, important decisions that would affect both the deployed military forces overseas and the people still living at home in the US. One day he was asked about this during an interview. The journalist pointed out that he was making life and death decisions for thousands of people on a daily basis, and making them quickly — how did he do it? Powell put it like this: "As a leader, you have to get comfortable making decisions without all the information at hand, so I have what I call a 40/70 rule. If I'm making decisions with less than 40% of the information, then I'm not educated enough to make a good decision. If I'm making a decision with more than 70% of the information, then I've waited too long and people will die." Damn. That last part really gets me every time. Most of us wait to make a decision until we have 95%, 98% or 100% of the information so we can be certain in our decisions. But the reality is waiting for that information, in his situation, will kill people. And for the rest of us, it will kill our dreams. Be honest. How much information do you need before you feel comfortable making decisions? For most of us, 70% is not enough.

'Analysis paralysis' and perfectionism are the biggest causes of inertia. We get stuck because we overthink everything or get cozy in a learning cycle, instead of committing to action and getting into a growth cycle. We all do this, myself included. Most of the time it's because we're avoiding making a decision that would lead us into action. So the Colin Powell rule is a tool to help us notice when we're overanalyzing everything when we should be getting into the action.

Never Reject Yourself

Why do we stop ourselves from taking action? We reject ourselves, before others ever get the opportunity to reject us. Imagine you're single (not hard to imagine if you are single), hanging out in a bar, and across the room you spot someone who is very attractive and appealing (or what some might call sexy AF). You're like, "Wow. I would like to get to know that person. Maybe date them. Maybe marry them!" But before you even finish that thought, you're in your own head. "That person is way too hot for me. Too outgoing, too cool, too much to ask for." You make a whole lot of assumptions about yourself, and reject yourself as being an option for that person before they even have a chance to reject you. But you know nothing about them! They might not reject you at all — and you've just talked yourself out of even saying hello.

By rejecting yourself, you have just guaranteed that you will not find out their name, you will not go on a date with them and you will definitely not get married to them. Before you rejected yourself, all those possibilities were on the table. So you've created this whole rejection scenario but it's not actually real. You've just rejected yourself before someone else can. But what would happen if you went up and introduced yourself? What if, in 5% of all the possible ways that this interaction unfolds, that the person is into you? What if there's a 5% chance you totally hit it off, and they say yes to that date? There's probably more than a 5% chance, honestly, but you will never know if you reject yourself.

This comes back to the fears of shame and judgement, which takes us right back to that big fear we talked about at the beginning of the book: social shaming. Rejection is a story that we tell ourselves, so if we go back to the cycle of outcomes, rejection is literally us telling ourselves a story about an imagined scenario. "If that person says no, that would mean I am unlovable. Then everybody will know I'm unlovable, and I'll be forever alone, living with my 11 cats." You can see that this is just a story, right? It's not reality.

There are just as many rejection stories around starting a business as there are around finding a partner. Anybody who's ever started a business knows it's going to be difficult. But if you try to play out the odds of whether it's going to work, you'll never even try. Let's use coaching, for example. You're really passionate about coaching, and you want to start a coaching business. But you don't know anybody who's done it, and you think that the odds of actually being able to do it and make a real living are minimal. You've heard stories of people trying to be coaches, not making any money from it and having to drive Uber to make ends meet. And even though you know of plenty of people making great money with coaching — people like Tony Robbins, Jack Canfield, and Zander Fryer — you reject the possibility that it could work for you. You know that it's possible, but you reject yourself as a successful and thriving coach. You talk yourself out of trying, even though deep down you want to have a life and a career that not only makes good money, but fulfills you.

But what could happen if you didn't reject yourself? What would your life look like if you decided that you were just going to go for it, full ass, and let the momentum carry you forward? Well, it would look like a life full of money, meaning and freedom, wouldn't it?

The Three R's

The final thing to know of the process of getting (and keeping) moving is that as you're working towards becoming successful, you're going to hear no. You're going to get beat up some days (metaphorically speaking). There will be days that you feel like you've been punched in the face — sometimes many days in a row. There are three Rs that you have to hang onto: resiliency, relentlessness and resourcefulness. I first learned these three Rs from a mentor of mine, Bedros Keuilian.

Bedros and his family came to the US to escape soviet controlled Armenia in 1980 and grew up having to dumpster dive to keep food on the table. Today Bedros is an Inc. 500 CEO, owns one of the fastest growing franchises in the world (FitBody Bootcamp) and is worth over $100 Million. He attributes a lot of his success of the years to these 3 Rs.

You have to become resilient in your pursuit. When you get knocked down, get up. When you hear no, try again. When something doesn't work, move on to the next experiment. Keep going, keep going, keep going. This is why having clarity is so important: it gives you a vision to hang onto. You know what outcome you're working towards, and it gives you the strength and willingness to keep on coming back for more.

You will have to be relentless. You will have to be tough. You will face obstacles and it will not be easy. Bedros says,

"When you expect life to be easy, life is hard. When you expect life to be hard, life actually gets pretty easy." So expect things to be tough. It becomes a lot more fun that way.

Finally, you need resourcefulness. According to Bedros, "In the absence of resources, you need to become resourceful." Everybody thinks you have to have money to make money. Everybody thinks that you have to have success to become successful. And this is, frankly, bullshit. There are so many stories of people coming up from nothing to have amazing lives. And what it all comes down to is resourcefulness. In the absence of resources, you must become resourceful. Everything is figure out-able, and if everything is figure out-able, it's just a matter of time. If you don't quit, and you're growing every day, success is the only possible outcome. You actually can't fail. It might take a little bit longer than you want, but you will get there.

NINE

DON'T FORGET TO THINK

"Insanity is doing the same thing over and over and expecting different results."

ALBERT EINSTEIN

Tony Robbins says that success requires massive action. And that's cool. But in my opinion, success requires massive action *plus reflection*. You can take all the action you want, but if you're running in the opposite direction to your goal, you're never going to get there. I'm not in the business of sending people into insanity, and so this chapter is designed to help you figure out how to take action and then review it in a meaningful way, so that you can trust yourself to adapt and succeed faster.

Review and Reflect

A couple of months after I quit my job at Cisco, I decided I was going to make a habit of doing something uncomfortable every single day. Some days it was something in my business, some days it was something to do with my health, some days it was something to do with my relationships. One day I called an ex-girlfriend that I had dated for two years and asked her to give me feedback on our relationship — I was using the 'review and reflect' practice on my romantic relationships. That was terrifying. Could you imagine calling an ex and asking 'what was the worst part about our relationship?' or 'how was I in bed?' ... yeah. That happened. It was one of the scariest things I've ever done. But I can tell you right now that the feedback I got in that conversation is the reason that today I'm married to the woman of my dreams. There's no question in my mind: without that conversation, I would not have my wife right now. I would not have this life right now. It was an incredibly uncomfortable 30-minute conversation, but in the end it was amazing. It revealed things about myself that I didn't want to admit, and some things I didn't know. It also revealed a ton to me about how little I knew about the opposite sex and the person I had been dating. That definitely drove home to me the power of 'review and reflect'. It gave me a ton of data to work with, and data is what we need.

Review and reflection is a crucial part of the growth cycle. If you never reflect, you can never course-correct. But it's also something that most people find very scary. Looking at the things that did not work out as planned is very uncomfortable and forces you to take responsibility where maybe you would prefer to ignore it. But remember: this is an opportunity to hang out in the growth mindset. If you get stuck in the fixed mindset, then every mistake or missed opportunity becomes your reality forever, but as we've said, it doesn't have to be like that. You can acknowledge where you messed something up, and start to look for ways to start fixing what's not working and moving forward.

All Data, No Drama

There are four types of feedback you can receive when you start to review and reflect. There is objective and subjective feedback, and then within each of those, there's internal and external feedback.

- Objective feedback is factual: whether you like it or not, there's no arguing with it. It's the truth and there's no way around it.
- Subjective feedback is emotional: it's driven by a feeling or an instinct. You can argue with it if you want, but it's going to keep presenting itself until you pay attention.
- External feedback comes from other people or the environment around you.
- Internal feedback comes from within yourself, either physically or psychologically.

All the data you will ever receive is some combination from these two sets.

So, for example, let's say I ate some of yesterday's sushi from the 7-11 down the road, and then a couple of hours later, I'm throwing up... out of both ends. That is objective internal feedback that I should not do that again. The data I get is that old convenience store sushi makes me sick and there's really no argument you can make that is going to change that fact.

What about subjective internal feedback? Well, you know that feeling when you go to work, and it makes you sick to do some of the things that you have to do every single day? That's internal subjective feedback telling you this probably isn't the life that you were meant to live.

Objective feedback might go back to the example of the two Johns in the sales role: if John A is making $50,000 and John B is making $200,000 in exactly the same circumstances, that's external objective feedback that John A is not doing something right. It won't tell him exactly what that thing is, but it gives him a chance to start investigating.

Subjective external feedback is your manager telling you that your work sucks. We get this kind of feedback all the time, but it's not objectively correct, and so our responsibility is to take the feedback, discern what's real and what's not, and then decide what we're going to do with it.

A note on subjective feedback: it's vulnerable to bias, the stories we have about yourselves, and other people's stories. You should absolutely be willing to ask people for feedback, but you don't have to accept it wholesale. Just because somebody says one thing does not make it factual truth. So, when I had that conversation with my ex-girlfriend, she gave me a ton of really good feedback... and then there was a little bit of feedback that was still tinged with a little bit of animosity, so I didn't necessarily need to take that stuff to heart.

If the feedback you're getting — either internally or externally — is objective, then run with it as fast as you can. Use that data as a way to start experimenting and figuring out how you can improve that data. But if you're getting subjective feedback — either internally or externally — run it through some filters. Is it actually true? Could it not be true? Could this just be a story? Can you act on it? Is it coming from a place of fear or a place of purpose?

If you're stuck figuring out if some data you're getting is objective or subjective, sometimes it just comes down to volume. There's an old saying: "If one person tells you you're drunk but you feel fine, ignore him. But if ten people tell you you're drunk, lay down." It's the same in business: let's say you have 100 clients, and 20 of them give you terrible feedback. Well that's probably objective. But if 99 clients give you glowing reviews and just one person gives you terrible feedback, that's probably subjective and you can take it with a grain of salt. That person might have just had a shitty day, maybe something rough is going on in their life and they're just taking it out on you. You never know. You just have to be able to figure out what kind of data you're really getting and then make an appropriate decision about what to do with it.

You can also take subjective feedback and try to turn it into objective feedback. While I was working on this section of the book, I interviewed Bedros Keuilian for my podcast. Bedros has been on over 500 interviews over the last few years. He was pretty sure our conversation was #536 — I'd say that makes him pretty well-qualified to give objective feedback on what makes a good interview. So I asked him, "On a scale of one to five, how was I as an interviewer?" He gave me a four and a half, so then I asked him what would I need to do to become a five. And then he gave me some concrete feedback on what would make me a five. Now, I trust his opinion more than somebody who's done two or three podcasts before, because he's been on over 500. He knows what's good, and what's not, and what really works for him and what he likes. So while that's technically subjective feedback, it's going to help me refine my objective ability as a podcast host.

Maddy and I also use this in our relationship. Every month, we do a review and reflection. We have a series of questions that we ask each other at the end of every month: on a scale of 1 to 10, how would you rank our relationship? And if it's not a 10, what would make it a 10? Or on a scale of 1 to 10, how do you feel about our physical intimacy? And if it's not a 10, what would make it a 10? On a scale of 1 to 10, how am I fulfilling your love languages? And so on. This helps us keep really connected to each other and ensures that the relationship stays healthy and growing.

The final thing when you're reflecting and reviewing on the data and feedback you've received is to be hyper-aware of the stories you tell yourself. It's so important to look at all of it with a bit of distance and perspective so that you don't miss really important stuff.

A good example around that came from a client of ours at High Impact Coaching. She was a health coach, and she was charging about $200 bucks per client per month. She had six clients, so she was making $1200 a month. When she started working with us, her goal was to make six figures per year in her coaching business, so we taught her how to increase her prices and charge $3000. The month after we had that conversation, she showed up to a call with me, and she goes, "Zander, I can't do this anymore. Nobody can afford $3000."

I thought, "Oh NO. Did we screw up her business?" But I wanted to dig into the data, so I asked her how many leads she got on the phone in the past month, and she said she had done 12 calls. So then I asked her at what price point she was trying to enrol her clients: $3000, as we had planned. Then I asked her how many of those 12 people she had enrolled, and she said four... and I was like, "Wait, what? You enrolled four people at $3000?" And she goes, "Yeah, 8 people could not afford this. No one can afford that much." Hold the phone, lady. Let's go back to the data here.

I told her to open her bank account and look at what she made last month and what she had made this month: $1200 vs $12,000. She started swearing and laughing, and I was like, "Of course, when you increase your price from $200 to $3000, you're gonna have less people who can afford it. But it's a story that no one can afford it." The factual data said that one out of three people could afford it — one out of three at twelve times the price. It's far better to enroll one in three people at twelve times the price than one in two people at a twelfth of the price. Right? So don't forget: rely on the data, not your stories. All data, no drama.

Comfort Crushing Challenge #3: Asking Critical Questions

Find two people that you really trust. Ask them, "On a scale of one to five, how would you rate our relationship?" Then, if it's not a five and you're feeling really brave, ask: "What would make it a five?"

Now: take the feedback with a grain of salt. But if you really trust them, it's probably going to be really good feedback.

Find two people that you really admire — people you know personally. It could be the same two people you asked the last question, or different people. Ask them how they see you limiting yourself. Find out where they see you getting stuck in your own stories or where you're not making the most of your opportunities.

This is about learning to ask yourself tough questions. I have all my clients ask themselves the following questions on a yearly basis:

- What were the good things that I did?
- What were the things that I didn't do?
- Who was I a year ago?
- Who am I now?
- What has changed and what hasn't?
- What do I need to fix moving forward?

- Where am I not standing up to what I need to be or the person I need to be to accomplish these goals?
- What am I doing right now, with my life?
- What am I spending a majority of time on in my life?
- Is that the path for me? Am I making this decision out of purpose, or am I making this decision out of fear?

These are all critical questions that I use to make sure that all my clients — and myself — are on the right path, doing the things we need to be doing.

If you can start to train your brain to critically question why you're doing things and how you're doing things, you're inevitably going to make better decisions. It stops you from falling into habitual thinking and getting stuck in your stories.

FxFxE

This exercise was developed by Cameron Herald, and it has been one of the most powerful tools that I've used. I implement it myself and with my team every single week to keep us on track towards our goals.

So you've set a goal. You've created a vision. How do you keep yourself on track?

Every single week, I ask myself, what's my percentage chance of achieving this goal? And the answer is my FxFxE: my focus, faith and effort.

Herald says you can quantitatively calculate the percentage chance that you will be successful in any endeavor, based on this equation. You take your focus, and you multiply it by your faith, and you multiply it by your effort.

It's a little bit subjective. But let's say, I was 50% focused on my goal, I have 50% faith that I can accomplish it, and I put in about 50% of my maximum effort. You don't come out with a 50% chance of success. If you remember tenth grade statistics, how do you multiply three percentages together? $0.5 \times 0.5 \times 0.5 = 0.125$. That's a 12.5% chance of success.

By half-assing it, you've basically guaranteed failure this week.

So if you want to guarantee success, you need to full-ass it every single week. You've got to find more faith, more focus and more effort if you want to really start moving towards your goals. I'm sharing this because since starting my business five years ago, I've accomplished 80% of my big, hairy, audacious goals. That's batshit crazy. Absolutely crazy. These are all massive goals that people are not usually able to accomplish in such short periods of time.

I'm talking about getting to $100,000 a month in my coaching business in 12 months. Meeting the woman of my dreams after six months of looking for her. Moving to a beautiful beach house in Encinitas. Getting a TED talk. Building a team of 15 people. Doubling the business every year (people love telling me you can't keep doubling a business, and I love proving them wrong).

The one reason I keep accomplishing 80% of the crazy things I put on my list is that I make sure that every week I'm keeping myself on track with my focus, faith and effort. If you want to get to an 80% success rate, $0.9 \times 0.9 \times 0.9 = 0.73$. So if you're bringing 90% faith, focus and effort, you're going to hit your goals about 73% of the time — close. Once you're at $0.95 \times 0.95 \times 0.95$, you're at 85%.

You have to have faith that you're going to get there — you really have to believe it. You have to focus — single-minded, relentless focus. And you have to put in effort — full-ass only.

Now, having 100% focus or effort does not mean that I

work 100 hours a week. I work about 40 hours a week, some-times 50 hours a week because I love what I do. But during those 40 or 50 hours, I don't half-ass anything. I'm full-ass, all the time. I'm 100% present during those 50 hours and then when I'm off, I'm off. Outside of work, I'm 100% present with my wife, or I'm 100% present in my self-development or I'm 100% present at the gym. I don't half-ass anything.

The Focus Rule of Squares

Since we just went through a tenth-grade math lesson, it'll make this principle easier to understand.

The goal for any entrepreneur is to create the most output possible. And your output is not a direct correlation of your focus, but a *squared* correlation of your focus.

So for example, if you have 100% focus, you will create 100% of the possible output. If you have 50% focus, what's 50% squared? Well, 0.5 x 0.5 = 0.25, so 50% squared is only 25%: if you split your focus evenly between two things,you'll actually only get 25% of the output on each. If you split your focus between three things, your output is down to about 11% on each thing. There's a Russian proverb that says if you chase two rabbits at once you will catch neither one — or if you prefer a modern version, if you try to shit on two toilets at once, things get messy — now we understand why.

We've talked about never half-assing anything and your focus is a big part of that. Whatever I'm doing, I'm 100% present for or I'm doing my best to be 100% present. If my focus is split, it will always hurt both things I'm doing. There's no such thing as multitasking. It's scientifically proven that your brain can only focus on one thing at a time. And that the transition period between doing different tasks — say, jumping between an email conversation and trying to get some deep work done — can be anywhere from five minutes to an hour, depending on what you're transitioning between. So if you're trying to jump between things, you'll be forever stuck in this lower state of 50% focus.

Focus doesn't mean that 100% of your time is focused on one single thing. It means that when you're working on something, it gets 100% of your attention until you're done. And in Part 4: Tactical Strategy, we're going to talk about how you can incrementally increase your focus and performance each week until you're really humming along.

TEN

TAMING THE DONKEYS

"We are what we repeatedly do. Excellence, then, is not an act, but a habit."

WILL DURANT

One of the most crucial components of learning how to execute on the stuff you need to get done is learning how to manage your own habits and behaviours.

In his book *Atomic Habits*, James Clear outlines the four components of a habit:

- You have a *cue* that triggers a desire.
- The *desire* elicits a behavior.
- The *behavior* leads to a reward.
- The *'reward'* — whether it's good or bad — is the outcome you end up with.

- As soon as you encounter that cue again, the whole cycle starts again.

This is the habit cycle, and the more often you go through it, the more ingrained the habit becomes in your brain.

Most of us have lots of habit cycles. We have habits around what we do each day, how we eat, how we use our bodies, what we think and so on. Habits are a foundational aspect of your behavior, and your behavior determines your progress, so getting your habits on the right track is super important. Thankfully, we can use the habit cycle to start to disintegrate bad habits and build good habits in their place — we can start to get those 95 donkeys in your subconscious mind pulling in the same direction as the 5 amazing horses.

The Sunflower Seed Incident

When I first read about the Habit Cycle in *Atomic Habits*, I immediately thought of one of my buddies from high school, Matt, who used to play baseball. When you play baseball, you sit in the dugout, waiting to get out on the field, and many teams chew sunflower seeds while they wait, then spit them out on the dirt while they're relaxing. Then when you're up to bat you head onto the field, strike out, then come back and chew some more sunflower seeds. So a few years ago, he and some of my other buddies were watching football one night at our friend Brian's house. Brian passed around some sunflower seeds, and sure enough Matt took a handful, and then spit them out on the carpet. Brian lost it. The rest of us thought it was hilarious. But the one thing that was obvious was that this was a completely automatic, subconscious behavior. He hadn't played baseball in years, but the sunflower seeds were a strong cue for him: The cue triggered the desire (to spit), and the behavior caused by that desire (the actual spitting) led to an outcome (the sense of relaxation). Of course, this behavior was totally out of place in our friend's living room, so the outcome was actually embarrassment, but you get the idea: habits get deeply ingrained in our brains, often so deep that we don't even notice them running there in the background.

Habit Hijacking

It's estimated that between 50 to 90% of all your actions are unconscious based actions. Do you clearly recall brushing your teeth this morning? Probably not — it just happened, because brushing your teeth is a habit. What about driving to work? When I lived in Los Angeles, I could drive an hour through traffic in a manual car, while drinking a coffee, talking on my hands-free and listening to music, all at the same time. Driving to work had become an unconscious habit, even though it's actually an incredibly complex thing to do. You're operating a 3000 or 4000 pound vehicle, and you're not even thinking about it. It's a bit scary. But a lot of our daily life is like this — we don't realize how much we do that's completely habitual.

The reason for this is evolutionary. As humanity evolved, our brains needed to offload conscious thought. Otherwise it would burn too much energy for us to feed it, and we would die from insufficient calories. We are evolutionarily programmed to not consciously think as much as we need to. This is how we ended up with so much subconscious activity, including the habits we build.

So if such a significant part of our actions are habit related, then habits are the most crucial part of becoming successful. Getting rid of any bad habits and creating good habits that will serve you as you're working towards your goals is absolutely key, because having the right habits saves you from having to make the same challenging decisions over and over again. It's like inserting little automatic programs in your brain that will just run behind the scenes if you put a little bit of time into programming them properly.

I have really doubled down on this, because I am actually an incredibly lazy person. I've just gotten really good at creating good habits, so that my laziness produces results. People think that being productive is hard work. They think that you're consciously putting effort into it all the time. And don't get me wrong, you're always putting in work. But once it becomes a habit, it becomes harder to *not* do the thing. Anybody who's really physically fit will tell you this: if you ask them whether it would be harder for them to go to the gym or not go to the gym, they will all tell you it's much harder to stay home. They've built the habit of going over a long enough period that it's actually more difficult to stop. Being efficient and productive is not just about working as hard as you can: it's about building the right habits that will take you where you want to go. work, if you focus on building the habit and it becomes automatic. I'll give you another example: I've woken up at 4 a.m. every morning for more than three years. And people think I'm crazy. But that habit is worn in now: I just pop out of bed now as soon as the alarm goes off. It just happens — I don't think about it. Maddy and I can go out and have a late night with friends and the next morning, BOOM. I'm up at 4. It wasn't easy in the beginning, but now that the habit is established, it's hard to stop.

Building And Breaking Habits

Once you realize that so many of your actions are dictated by your subconscious, then you realize that you have control. You know that you can shape your subconscious, which means that you have control of whether your habits are useful or destructive. Of course, doing this goes back to taking 100% ownership: if you can acknowledge that you are constantly being trained by your environment and that habits are taking hold whether or not you're consciously directing them, you can start to get to work. As you notice all the habits that are 'bad' — the ones that are not going to help you get to your goals — you can start to unwind them and replace them with good habits that will support your journey. And as soon as you start to do that, life gets more simple and easy.

Let me introduce you to Aspen.

Not only is he the cutest puppy ever (bias? What bias?), he is also a great example of how the Habit Cycle is created. When we first got Aspen, his habit cycle swung into action almost immediately. We would get his food out, it would clink into his bowl and he would come running. At first he was getting massively overexcited about food, so we'd stop moving, and have him go sit on his bed. Once he had settled, we'd finish making the food and then bring it to him. So he learned very quickly that the cue (the sound of his food) triggers his desire (to eat the food). He figured out that if he adjusted his behavior in response to that desire (going straight to his bed instead of harassing us), that he would get a better reward (getting to eat his food sooner). So now when we start to get his food out, he runs to his bed and waits patiently

Now, we'd all like to think we're a bit more advanced than our dogs... but really we're all on the same spectrum. Most of us have habit cycles just like Aspen does. The cue might be getting home from work, which triggers a craving to relax and disconnect. The response is to grab a beer or pour a glass of wine and plonk down on the couch with Netflix. The reward is feeling some relief after the day. That's a habit cycle right there, and that's how most of our habits are built. It's often pretty mindless. It's the same at the other end of the day: waking up acts as a cue. It triggers a craving to see what's happening on social media. Your behavior is to grab your phone and start scrolling, which rewards you with a little dopamine boost. It's easy to see how that becomes a habit, right? But now you're basically programming yourself into being a dopamine fiend every morning.

Reconfiguring Your Habits

I'm not going to tell you that you can never have a wine after work, no more Netflix, no more social media for you. It's not realistic and it's also not necessary: a little bit of indulgence can add a lot to your quality of life — you've just gotta do it mindfully, so that you're in charge of your behaviors, not your autopilot subconscious. So maybe you save the wine for Friday night, limit your Netflix time to a specific window, and hold off on social scrolling until you've gotten your curated morning routine out of the way.

The easiest way to unpick habits that are not serving you is to start with the cue. Don't mess around with trying to moderate the intensity of the habit — go straight to the source. For example, when we decided we were going to quit bingeing Netflix, we did three key things: we got rid of the visual cue of the TV, we physically limited our access, and we introduced accountability. Removing the visual cue meant taking the TV out of our bedroom. It's out of sight, out of mind. Restricting our access meant that we started turning off the WiFi at a specific time each night. That means that if we want to watch something, we have to make an active decision, and one of us has to go upstairs and turn it back on — we can't just mindlessly turn on Netflix like we used to. Finally, I also gave Maddy carte blanche permission to hold me fully accountable, consequences and all, if I watched more than two episodes of anything in a week. All three of these changes simply introduced hurdles. The hurdles make it harder for me to start the habit cycle, and so it naturally happens less often.

But what about making new habits easier? Again, there are three things you can do:

- Adding cues
- Stupid-proofing your habits
- Rewarding good behavior.

Let's say you want to read more before bed: adding a visual cue might mean keeping your book visible. Keep it on the night-stand, so it's impossible for you to miss. Then you can stupid-proof the behavior you want: set a specific amount of pages you want to read each day, and keep a running tally of how you're doing with it. I keep a list of the different books I want to read and how many pages I want to get through each night. And then I reward good behavior. Personally, I get a dopamine hit when I get to buy a book I want, so every time I finish a book, I get to buy the next one, and that gives me a good feeling that makes me want to trigger that habit cycle more often.

Environmental Design

Your environment has a massive impact on your habits, because your environment is full of cues that can trigger useful habits or destructive ones. Your environment dictates your destiny, but you dictate your environment.

If you're taking full ownership over your life, you have the ability to change your environments. It's not necessarily easy, but it is true. A study of returning Vietnam veterans found that a huge number of those people — as many as 20% — reported being addicted to heroin while they were on active duty there. But when they got home, that number dropped massively — only 5% of the people who had been addicted abroad had become re-addicted when they came home.[1] This was a shocking discovery for the medical community, because 90% of heroin addicts coming out of rehab would quickly relapse. But the opposite thing happened with the Vietnam vets. As soon as they came home, their rate of addiction plummeted, and it was all about the cues they were receiving. Being in a highly traumatic war zone was a cue to seek relief, which kicked off a habit cycle of heroin use. But back home, where the cues were not so extreme, the habit cycle rarely ever got started up again. The opposite was true for people leaving rehab: in the rehab center, all the cues that started their heroin use habit cycle were gone. The triggers weren't there, and so they could stop using. But as soon as they went home, all the cues and triggers that had got them addicted in the first place came right back into action, and so it was almost impossible to avoid the habit cycle starting back up again.

There are seven different types of environment, and you have control over all of them:

1. Your intellectual environment: what's going on in your brain
2. Your emotional environment: how you're feeling about yourself and your life
3. Your spiritual environment: your connection with faith or a higher purpose
4. Your physical environment: your physical body, your health and sense of wellbeing
5. Your relational environment: the quality of all your relationships
6. Your natural environment: the physical area or location you exist in
7. Your financial environment: how your money is being used and managed

Each of these environments dictates your ability to succeed in different ways, and they influence you in different ways.

The Seven Environments

Time for another exercise: go through the list of these seven environments and write down everything that comes to mind for each one. When you're done, go through and make a note on each thought or idea you wrote out: is this positive or negative? Does this thought or reaction support your goals, or does this detract from your goals?

Once you've scored everything, go through each environment and start making decisions. You can keep it the way that it is, you can increase something, you can decrease something, or you can completely get rid of it. Whatever you decide, start making conscious decisions around your environments, rather than allowing your environments to just happen to you. This might take some time, and that's okay, but put your list somewhere that you will see it and keep working on it.

The hardest one to change here is your relational environment. Jim Rohn says that we're all the average of the five people you spend the most time with. Clients always tell me, "I can't change my family and friends." But the reality is that you can. You'll always be related to your family, but if they cause you more harm than good, you do not have to spend your time with them. And the reality is that you can change your friends — you're just choosing not to, because it's scary. I get it. But when you let go of relationships that are not serving you, new ones that do serve you will come up in their place. This is why I have a rule of threes when it comes to my relational environment: I have three-day people, three-hour people and three-minute people.

Three-day people are people that inspire me, people that motivate me, people that are critical thinkers, people that are doing the things that I want to do. They're impacting the world. They're making tons of money, they have great family relationships and they have free time to travel and do the things that matter. These are the people that I can spend an entire weekend with and come out feeling higher-level than I was before.

There's three-hour people that you could spend three hours with, and maybe you enjoy having dinner with them or hanging out for drinks. They might have a lot of positive qualities, but maybe there's some things that they're still figuring out, and while they're fun, they're not super inspirational. And then there's three-minute people. These are the people that maybe you were friends or acquaintances with in the past. Maybe you're happy to catch up with them at a party for a few minutes, but you don't want to spend a few hours with them, because they're not the people you want influencing you.

This is hard. It's always going to be hard. I have a buddy who used to be a three-day person, and over the years, I've had to acknowledge that he should be more of a three-minute person now. He's not moving forward with his life, with his health, and while I want to keep motivating him, I can't go out on benders with him like I used to. I want to make sure I'm spending enough time with him to pull him up with me, but I can't spend three days with him. I want to influence him, not the other way around.

All the other environments are incredibly important, but your relational environment might be the most important of all of them, because it can dictate a lot about the other ones. So really take careful account of your relational environment, the people you spend time with, and the people you allow into your world to affect your subconscious mind.

That's not to say that you should skim over the other environments. Your physical body is an environment that you live in. People wonder why they're not successful, but if they're not taking care of the one body that they're given to move through this world, how can they expect to have the energy, the mental focus, and the stamina to accomplish the things that they want in life?

Your financial environment is also something you can dictate. You don't have to be at the mercy of your money. You don't have to exist forever in a feast-or-famine cycle of having enough cash and then having none. You can start to put structures in place — like a debt repayment plan, savings, retirement planning, investment plans — to start to stabilize your financial environment. You can put time and effort into your own business and learn the skills to make more of an income as well. Remember what Bedros said: "In the absence of resources, get resourceful" and get to work. It takes time, but this will bring a lot of peace and confidence to your life.

Same thing with your emotional environment and your intellectual environment — the thoughts you think, the emotions you feel, these are subconscious programming and often completely habitual. We've already established you need to take ownership over that, because the thoughts you think and the emotions that you feel are going to dictate the actions you take, and therefore the results.

Your natural environment is also key: the best quote of all time comes from my mama, when she yelled at me in the tenth grade: "How can you expect to get anything important done when your room looks like shit?!" You can't, and most of us have so much physical and mental clutter to deal with that in the next chapter, we're going to dive deep into how you can get it all under control. But before we do that, we need to figure out what truly motivates us and kicks us into action, no matter what the environment around us is like.

The Carrot and the Stick

"Zander, I've done a lot of personal growth. I don't really like the idea of dangling a carrot in front of me or waving a stick behind me to keep me motivated and taking action," said one of our clients Tina on a group coaching call.

I smiled and calmly replied "Tina, do you meditate?

"Yes I do. I have been for years."

"Amazing. About how many times a week do you start to levitate off the ground while meditating? It doesn't have to be an exact number, just give me a rough estimate." I said with a completely straight face.

"Uhh, zero," she laughed.

I smiled back, "The moment you begin to levitate off of the ground, is the moment you have completely conquered the ego and the control of your subconscious mind. Until then your subconscious still dictates the majority of your actions and you need tools like accountability to keep you motivated and moving. So you can either stay stuck where you are at, or get the f*ck over yourself."

Accountability is the relational environment part that really allows you to accomplish these things. Accountability is the string that holds everything you're trying to do together. Accountability is one of the most pivotal things to help you achieve your goals, and anybody who thinks they're beyond it is an idiot.

We all like to believe we're beyond needing the carrot or the stick to drive us forward (the carrot being a positive motivator or reward, such as a holiday or bonus if you hit your goal, and the stick being a negative motivator or punishment, like having to do something embarrassing if you don't hit the goal). But none of us are beyond accountability. The day you're meditating and you start to levitate off the ground, you no longer need accountability. At that moment, your mind is so powerful that you will absolutely be able to do whatever you want, without any help from anyone else. Until that day, get over yourself. You are not there yet, and the 95% of your brain that's subconscious will always be calling the shots until you learn to wrangle it. And to do that, you need help. Just like everybody else.

There's no such thing as a self-made entrepreneur. Nobody has ever gotten there on their own. It will never happen in the existence of creation. We all need other people — their skills, their experience, and their inventions. It's not a failure to accept this. It's humility, and wisdom: to acknowledge to yourself, and to others, that you're not good enough yet, but you want to be, and so you're going to seek and accept help. The only way you can create the life you want is to get comfortable being uncomfortable. And how do you do that? You have someone hold you accountable to doing the uncomfortable things, which leads to growth, which leads you to you becoming that person. But it all starts with accountability.

Like I said, I am not beyond needing this. I have never levitated for even one second of my life (and believe me, I've tried). When I quit my job at Cisco, I realized that up until that point, accountability had been baked in: our parents hold us accountable all throughout our lives. Our teachers hold us accountable in school. Our coaches hold us accountable in sports. When we're in a nine-to-five, we have a supervisor to hold us accountable for getting everything done. Literally everything in life has been programming my subconscious (and yours) from Day One to rely on accountability. But now, the first time I was actually going to go after something in life, purposefully, for the first time, accountability was the one thing I no longer had.

Over the next year, I spent tens of thousands of dollars on coaching and accountability. I gradually figured out that the stick works much better for me than the carrot: having to 'fess up to someone I admire that *no, I did not do the thing you told me to do* is much more motivating to me than *if I do this, then I can reward myself.* That's me, but both work: you have to figure out what works best for you. Either way, you need someone in your life who is going to hold you to getting it all done.

Let me give you an example. Back in 2017, I sat in on a workshop with Craig Ballantyne, who is an amazing coach, entrepreneur and close friend of mine. He's helped nearly 300 people become millionaires in his career, so he knows a thing or two. I loved his approach, so I started doing weekly account-ability with him afterwards. That was the year my business really started taking off. In the workshop, he also helped me get clear on a personal goal of mine. I had been incredibly single for about four years at that point, and one of my goals was to meet an amazing woman by the end of that year. October 2017 rolls around and I still haven't met anyone. I went to three weddings in six weeks, and when I came home I sent Craig an email, saying how fun it had been to see all my friends falling in love and getting married. He emailed me back right away: "You know, one of your goals for 2017 was to meet an amazing woman. What are you doing about that?" He was holding me accountable. *Damn.* I had been so focused on the business that dating hadn't really been a priority for me, and I told him that. When I got his reply, it said just two words: "Public account-ability."

Well, go hard or go home, right? I went to my Facebook group of 2,500 business owners who had worked with me. And fired up a Facebook Live titled "Help Me Find Love". I told everybody: "My goal is to meet an amazing woman by the end of 2017, and I have 60 days left to do it. If I don't do it, I will do whatever weird shit you guys come up with".

It. Blew. Up.

There were droves of comments. *Dance on Third Street Promenade naked. Shave your head. Donate your car. Fly me to Mexico.*

Now, this is a group full of coaches. Lots of them wanted to tell me that I just needed to work on myself and trust that the right person would come along. But I'd been doing that for over four years, and now it was time for action.

Fortunately, because I put myself out there, a lot of people started reaching out to me, saying "Hey, I want to introduce you to my cousin/best friend/sister/daughter." I went on a bunch of dates, and it was good to get moving, but nothing really came from it.

But then, a few weeks later, a girl from Australia reached out. And she just said, "Hey, I don't know what could come from this, but I saw your Facebook Live and I'm just really attracted to your energy and everything that you're doing. I'd love to connect. Would you be open to a Zoom call?" So we hopped on a Zoom, really connected, I fell in love with her accent, and we set up a second date.

Now, the way Maddy tells it, I forgot what time it was and I stood her up on the second date — and though I'll never admit it, that may have been true. Luckily, she was also at a point where she knew she needed to take action, so she reached back out to me and was like, "Look, nothing's gonna come from this unless we meet in person. I'm heading to Dubai to spend the holiday with my dad, but what if I stop over in San Diego on the way?" I was like, "Because San Diego and Dubai are right next to each other?!"

Of course, I said yes. She was supposed to come for three days, and ended up staying for a whole week. We dated long-distance for ten months after that, and then she relocated to the US. We have now been together for four years and happily married for two of them. But we met and fell in love two days before the end of 2017 — just 48 hours before my deadlines and all the crazy 'sticks' would have started whacking me. And it's all thanks to some public accountability.

Like I said before: you have to figure out whether the carrot or the stick works for you. Personally, I think the stick works much better for the majority of people — though most won't want to admit it — and that's why whenever one of our clients has something they absolutely must get done but they just can't seem to make it happen, we'll have them do a public account-ability post. They go to the High Impact Coaching Facebook group, just like I did, and post: "I will post my video sales letter/write the piece of copy/schedule the call by close of business Friday, or I will send $100 to the first five people who comment on this post." Obviously, they're going to get a bunch of comments on that post, so that would be $500 if they don't finish it on time. You're a lot more likely to finish it on time if you have five people holding you accountable — they're gonna be chomping at the bit to get that $100 from you, so now you have five people keeping you socially accountable to actually making something happen. Believe me, it works.

If there's no one in your life right now who can hold you accountable, the Internet is full of people who are waiting to meet you. There are more Facebook groups for this kind of thing than you can imagine. Find the community, find the environment, and ask. Ask people to be a part of your accountability circle, find an accountability buddy. You can join a mastermind for group social accountability, either paid or free. You could start a mastermind of your own (and if you've never heard of a mastermind before, it's a group of like-minded people who meet regularly, brainstorm with each other, and hold each other accountable to what each person says they're going to do). You can hire a coach, either individually or as part of a group. I'm a huge fan of anything paid, because people who pay, pay attention.

Back in 2018 I hired Bedros Keuilian, who I mentioned earlier. I hired him for a year and paid him $50,000 for it. He's a very intimidating guy. Lovely, but scary as hell. Huge, very masculine, very successful dude. Now, I don't get intimidated. I used to work with C-level executives at Disney and NBC. None of them ever intimidated me. But Bedros scares the shit out of me. I already knew most of what he was going to tell me to do — I just wasn't doing it. So I hired him because he's so scary that if I tell Bedros I'm going to do something, and I don't do it... it freaks me out too much to even think about it. I did every single thing he told me to do. One of the best $50,000 I ever spent.

Today I've spent close to $500,000 on my own account-ability and coaching, being part of masterminds and various communities that keep me accountable to do the shit that I say I'm going to do. This might sound crazy, but this is investing: you're investing in your own abilities, your own future, and you're committing to doing the uncomfortable things which are so powerful and will take you so far.

You don't have to invest hundreds of thousands of dollars when you first start, but you should invest enough that it makes you a little queasy when you do it. That's how you know you are pushing past your comfort zone.

Whatever accountability route you choose, make sure it's someone you deeply do not want to disappoint, and set it up so that it's non-invasive. Make it easy to work accountability into your day. My first accountability buddy was my friend Garrett. Right after AJ died, we agreed that we would text each other every day to say whether or not we had done our mindset work. I really did not want to add any more disappointment to Garrett in that time, so I was highly motivated to get it done, and sending a text that just said *MSWD* (for 'mindset work done') made it completely non-invasive, but it was enough to cue me to kick off my mindset work habit cycle each day.

What is the definition of success? It's being able to do the things and accomplish the things that most others can't or won't. That's what success is. The goal is to be better than the average. To surpass what's popular and easy. Accountability is not popular and some days it is not easy. But if you want this life with more money, more freedom and more meaning, you have to do something different than what's popular. You have to go beyond what everyone else is willing to do, and whether it's the carrot or the stick, you are going to need accountability tools to constantly push you outside of your comfort zone to get there.

---

1. *Addiction*, (1993) 88, 1041-1054, "Vietnam veterans' rapid recovery from heroin addiction: a fluke or normal expectation?", by Lee N. Robins. http://dok.slso.sll.se/CPF/journal_clubs/j.1360-0443.1993. tb02123.x.pdf

TACTICAL STRATEGY

This is the part of the book where we get down to the tools, tactics and routines that, in my experience, are going to empower you to create the business — and life — that you really want.

The most important thing to remember when you're actually getting down to the level of taking specific action is that productivity and busy-ness are not the same thing. Everybody's busy. Not very many people are productive. We all have the same 24 hours in a day, so how come some people accomplish so much, while some others accomplish so little? It has less to do with how many things you get done in a day and more to do with whether you're doing the right things.

A big part of productivity is having clarity about what you're doing, where you're going and how to make sure you stay focused. I think of productivity like a speedboat: if you want to make a speed boat go faster, there's two ways to do it. You can give the speedboat a bigger engine, or you can offload all the unnecessary weight. You can make it more powerful, or you can make it lighter, and what we're going to do here is learn how you can do both.

Clarity helps you streamline what you're working on, so that you can offload all the stuff that might seem important to begin with, but is actually unnecessary. And the strategies we're going to cover for the rest of the book are how you make your engine more powerful so that you can get more of the right stuff done.

ELEVEN

GETTING SHIT DONE

"Focus on being productive instead of busy."

TIM FERRISS

Before I left Cisco I was the second-ranked salesperson in a 1200-person organization. And technically I was an engineer, not a salesperson. And I was 20 years younger than anyone else in the top 50.

Everyone always thought I had some genius sales tactics I was using to pull in $15 million, $20 million and $30 million deals. But the truth was I actually wasn't even that great at sales.

I was just really good at being productive.

Ever since my days at UCLA, balancing the AirForce ROTC, my engineering course load, duties as the president of a fraternity, and 20 hours a week of part-time work, I learned there was a huge difference between being busy and being productive.

Pareto's Principle (a.k.a. the 80/20 rule) teaches us that 80% of the outcome can be produced by 20% of the effort.

When I was at Cisco, I had the territory of three account managers instead of one. So I focused on the top 20% that produced 80% of the outcome for each. Let's do the math

I worked around 60% as much as everyone else (around 35 hours a week while others were working 45-50) but I produced 240% of what others were producing — simply by learning how to be more productive and less busy.

Today, companies hire me for $2000 a session to teach their employees what I am about to share with you in the rest of this chapter.

In this chapter, we're going to cover my favorite productivity strategies. They're not hacks, they're not designed to guarantee to you a working week of just a few hours — they're the tools that people at the top of their game use to make meaningful progress on the most important components of their business.

Craig Ballantyne, my friend and mentor I mentioned before, says that structure equals freedom. A lot of people fear structure, but structure is the platform for us to launch from. Far from restricting us, structure gives us a foundation to help us to stay focused on what really matters. Without it, we struggle, we're overwhelmed, we don't know what to do. We don't know where to think. Structure is really important for us.

Is It Urgent or Important?

So now that we know that 80% of your results come from 20% of your actions, it's time to figure out which tasks are going to get you that big result and which ones you can delegate or delete. Every task fits into four categories:

- Urgent and important: do it now
- Important but not urgent: plan when you're going to do it
- Urgent but not important: delegate this, don't do it yourself
- Not urgent and not important: eliminate this altogether

Let's take a look at some common tasks as a starting entrepreneur, to see where they fall in this matrix:

- Scheduling your next sales call: urgent and important. You need to be the one to do it, and it's key that it happens soon.
- Designing next month's social media posts: important, not urgent. It's gotta get done, but the deadline is a long way off.
- Answering all your emails: Urgent, not important. Email often feels like a big priority, but most of the time, it's a distraction from the tasks that would actually move your business forward. Yes, sometimes there will be a legitimately urgent or important email, but it's rare.
- Scrolling through social media: not urgent and not important. This can happen in downtime when all the stuff that will make a real difference to your business is done.

When you first start working on applying this quadrant to your own tasks, you want to focus on the first two options as much as you possibly can. Over time, as you get the hang of assessing which tasks fall into which category, you should be able to start to shift towards focusing more on the second type: important but not urgent. All the urgent stuff should get taken care of so that you can start to find more space and time to deal with the things that are going to create a big result, without creating a lot of stress too.

Overwhelm happens when we're trying to keep all these tasks in our head at once — if you've ever thought, "Oh shoot, I need to remember to..." you know what I'm talking about. Your brain is trying to juggle masses of information, which leaves no room for creativity, critical thinking and decision-making, so a key part of learning to get more shit done is to get all these tasks and to-dos out of your head and onto a page somewhere so that your brain can focus on more important things. And that's where we come to the GSD List.

The Get Shit Done List

Are you ready to get super tactical? Cool, let's do it.

Meet the Get Shit Done List: you get everything out of your head onto one single list and then start to make decisions on that list. I first learned this idea from David Allen and his "Getting Things Done" framework. You might take action on a task right away, you might keep a task on the list, you might put it on a secondary list to think about in six months, or you might say no to it and just get rid of it.

You will be updating this list every day. Every night in your evening bookend (which we will get to shortly) you might add some things to the list and choose the top 5 tasks to add to a "daily to-do list" for the next morning. That way you are constantly working on only the things that will produce the biggest results.

Make sure you put everything down on this list so that you don't end up with a huge pile of messes and incompletes that will take ages to deal with every few months. Do it daily if you have to. Put everything down: enrolling the kids in swimming lessons, buying the new chair for your office, calling that potential client. Look for the most high-impact tasks that will legitimately move your business forward and choose those to be your big slimy frog for each day (no, buying a new chair is not high-impact. Calling the client though? Now you're talking).

If there's stuff on your GSD List that will take two minutes or less, just do it. Knock it off — even if it's difficult. Send the big invoice. Reply to the tricky email. It will take you so little time and give you back so much mental bandwidth.

Write down every place in your life that there is mess, clutter or unfinished task — anything you need to do or make a decision on. Anything at all in...

- Your house
- Your relationship
- Your kids
- Your friends
- Your family
- Your health
- Your business

Now under each section list out the different things that you need to do — all the loose ends you need to tie up.

- I need to vacuum the living room
- I need to get a new picture frame for our wedding photo
- I need to fix the squeaky wheel on my chair

- I need to call Katy about the new report that just came in
- I need to clean the oil stain in the garage
- I need to talk to my wife about planning our next vacation

List it all out. Get it out of your head and onto a piece of paper then leave it alone for 24 to 48 hours.

When you come back to it, 24 to 48 hours later, see if you can get even more things out — anything you forgot or ignored the first time around. Then go to the top of the list and work your way down, making a note of how long each one would take, whether it's five minutes, two hours, three days, ten weeks, whatever it is.

Once you're finished noting down the times, schedule an hour to come back and go through the list so you can make a decision on what to do about each remaining item. (And remember — if it takes less than two minutes, stop with the list and just get it done, then come back and keep going.)

When you get to your scheduled hour, you have a few options about what to do with each item. You can keep it on the list, you can put it on your calendar to make some specific time to do it. You can take it off the list and add it to a Tickler File (as in, it tickles your fancy, but it's not for right now), or you can decide to scratch it off the list altogether and be done with it — you can feel confident that you've thought about it, and the answer is no, you're not going to do this thing.

This exercise is incredibly freeing. Some stuff just needs quick action, some stuff needs a longer decision, some stuff is never going to happen. But no matter what, it all needs to be dealt with. Cleaning up your mental and physical environment will be a huge support as you start working towards everything that you want to be doing.

The Daily GSD

The GSD gives you an incredibly focused to-do list to work from.

Each night before I finish working I go to my GSD list and choose the three to five items that will have the biggest result and turn them into my to-do list for the day ahead.

(I don't choose 10 or 15, because if I only get through 5, I'm gonna feel shitty about it, even though those were big important tasks that I should feel good about completing. If I get through all 5 and I'm only halfway through the day, I can go back to my GSD list and get a few more.)

Out of those high-impact items, I make a note of the one thing that is going to be the most difficult or demanding and I schedule that in my calendar for first thing in the morning. That way, if it's the only thing I get done all day, the day will have been a success. This is also known as 'eating the slimy frog', and we'll talk about that more in a second.

Once I've got my most important task scheduled, then I'll write up a note with the three to five tasks that I want to get done so I can see when I get to my desk in the morning. Then I'll make my 'yes/no/later' decisions on any tasks that have been added to my GSD List throughout the day, and then I'm done.

You know why I do this at night, and not in the morning? It's because I don't want my brain thinking about everything that needs to happen the next day and messing with my sleep. If you get all this planning out of your head and onto a notepad or document, you'll sleep better, and you'll be more focused and ready to get going when you start work in the morning.

Book-Ending Your Day

This strategy comes from Darren Hardy's book, *The Compound Effect*. While you can almost never control everything in the middle of your day, you have control over how it starts and ends.

Throughout the day, all kinds of things can happen: one of your systems breaks, an employee will call you for help with a problem they're facing, you'll get a flat tire on the way to the office, your kid bites someone at school, your husband bites someone at work — there are so many things that are completely out of your control throughout the day. But what you can control are the activities you do when you first wake up in the morning, and right before you go to bed.

That makes those two windows the most crucial time periods in the day.

Everybody talks about the morning routine being absolutely paramount, and while the morning routine is important, I think the evening routine is even more important. Whatever you're doing for the last 45 minutes before you go to bed is what's having the deepest effect on your subconscious mind. If you watch zombie movies before you go to bed, then for the next 8 or so hours, you're marinating on violence and fear, so it's no wonder if you wake up feeling stressed and anxious. But if you read, snuggle with your partner or do some gentle stretches before you go to bed, there's a good chance you wake up feeling calm and refreshed, having just had 8 hours immersed in that blissed-out state.

What you do right before you go to bed and what you do first thing in the morning are the two most crucial things for making the most of each day, and we call these windows the book ends. They bookend your day to start and finish as you want it to.

When you're designing your book ends, start simple. You don't have to overdo it. It took me years to build to the book ends that I currently have. Work backwards: start by thinking about what you want your morning routine to be, and then create an evening routine that supports that.

For example, my morning routine is to wake up at a specific time every day. I don't care what time you choose, but choose a time and stick to it. Do not break that arrangement with yourself. Do not hit snooze when your alarm goes off. Your subconscious works with agreements. So if you tell your subconscious you're gonna wake up at 7am, and then snooze until 7:35, you're teaching your subconscious mind that your conscious mind is not reliable and can't be trusted.

So when you say to your subconscious, "I'm going to go start this new business and I'm going to be successful", your subconscious goes, "No, you're not, you liar. You can't even wake up at 7. How the hell could you start a business? You can't even get up on time, how are you gonna make a million dollars?"

How you start your day is how you run your day. And if you start your day off with a lie to yourself, the rest of your day is going to be very, very difficult. You're always going to be behind, you're always going to be chasing, you're always going to feel a little bit overwhelmed. I honestly couldn't tell you the last time that I hit snooze. Years and years ago. It's crazy how much this one habit has affected my life. This is the foundation for everything else that unfolds, so if nothing else, get this right. Pick a time to wake up, and get up at that time.

Now, as for what the rest of your morning book-end might look like, it's going to be different for everybody. For example, Maddy's morning routine is very different from mine, because she has a totally different energy to me. Her morning routine is softer and a little bit more flowy, while mine is very rigid and hard-charging.

However you put yours together, your morning routine should accomplish three things:

1. Do something that's hard.

If you're not used to going to the gym, go to the gym first thing. If you're trying to work on meditation, make meditation the first thing. For me right now, it's getting in the cold plunge pool every single morning to get my nervous system going and to boost my immune system. I hate it. I hate it every single morning. It scares me every single morning. But I do it first thing, then it's out of the way and I'm lit up afterwards.

The thing that feels hard will change for you over time. For example, I love going to the gym now that I've been going for many years. It comes easy to me now, and it even feels like a reward, so I put it off until later in the day once I've gotten some harder stuff out of the way. So stay mindful of what is actually going to challenge you first thing in the morning, and adjust your routine over time as these changes gradually happen.

2. Eat the slimy frog.

If you've never heard this analogy before, let me break it down for you real quick.

Let's say you have a to-do list for the day with five items on it, one of which is to eat a big, slimy frog. Gross, I know.

Most people would do the other tasks first, putting off the horrible moment of having to eat the big slimy frog, right? You go do all the smaller easier things, but that means that all day, you're dreading the moment of eventually having to eat the frog. So you put it off and put it off until it gets late, you're tired, and you can justify putting it off until tomorrow. And then tomorrow the same thing happens, and the frog never gets eaten.

Even if it's the task that would make the biggest possible difference to your progress, you never do it, because it's the task you most fear.

So if you get out of bed and eat the frog (send the scary email to a potential client, make the tough phone call, create the content or whatever it is) right there at the start of the day, you're free. Free from worry, free from stress, and the rest of the day is easy.

You feel accomplished, you feel like you've done something good, which gives your brain a hit of dopamine and norepinephrine, which is basically the chemical combination for motivation. That hormonal effect will affect you for the rest of the day and keep you moving through all the other, easier stuff you have to get done.

If you do the scariest task first, the rest gets easier.

3. MOVE YOUR BODY.

When I wake up, I chug an entire bottle of water with a little bit of lemon and ginger in it, just to flush out my system and rehydrate. Then I do five minutes of breath work and yoga just to get the body moving, because your lymphatic system has just been settled for the last seven or eight hours, and you want to get that moving, get your blood circulating again, so that your brain gets a bit more oxygenated and a bit more alert and ready to get busy. Once I'm done with my yoga and breathwork, I meditate, then I go do the cold plunge.

I climb out of the cold plunge, rug up, and then get straight to eating my frog. I do not do anything else — I don't check email, I don't check social or read the news or do anything but get straight to work and spend 90 minutes on that one important thing. If I did nothing else for the entire day, this morning routine would make me feel successful.

As a side note, there are all kinds of reasons that people feel like they can't control their mornings — they've got kids, a dog, they're still working 9-to-5, whatever it is. This comes down to 100% ownership again. Set the boundaries you need to set so that you can have the 30 or 60 minutes you need in the morning, because if you can't do that, the rest of your day is always going to be a shambles.

When it comes to the evening routine, the number one thing I suggest is a brain dump — getting all the to-do list items out of your head — just like you did with the Get Shit Done list. The more stuff you try to store in your brain, the more overwhelmed you'll feel. We just don't have enough space in our working memory to hang onto every single thing we all need to do every day, and so as soon as you get them out of your brain and onto a piece of paper, you will instantly feel psychological relief.

So I get everything out, and then do what I call a brag book, also called a gratitude journal. It's simple: write down five things that you're grateful for, five things you accomplished during the day, and one thing you can improve upon. This allows you to live more in a state of gratitude, because the big accomplishments only happen every now and then, and we all need a bit more motivation to keep us going.

We're five times more likely to be programmed by negative than we are to be programmed by positive. We need five things that make us feel grateful and like it's all worth it, and we need five things we've accomplished today to remind us that we're making progress even when it doesn't feel like it. These accomplishments can all be simple things: I woke up to my alarm. I made an awesome omelet for breakfast, I had a difficult conversation with my significant other, I enrolled that client, I just reached out to another client, I went to the gym — it's about just celebrating the action steps you're taking to remind your subconscious that you're being successful.

Then find a way to disconnect from the day in a healthy way. A big glass of wine and Netflix is not usually the answer. Watching TV actually tends to turn your brain back on, and booze is going to interfere with your sleep quality. So, an Epsom salt bath, a meditation, reading a good fiction book with a positive story to program the brain (*The Alchemist* by Paulo Coelho and *Tuesdays With Morrie* by Mitch Albom are two great options). A lot of people don't understand the importance of sleep. We've all heard about successful people who only sleep for three or fours hours a night, and yes — there are some people who sleep that little and are wildly successful, but they are few and far between and they get Alzheimer's pretty damn quickly.

The high majority of the most successful people sleep and sleep well. I was talking to my buddy Rob Dial, who is another bad-ass coach and host of the Mindset Mentor Podcast — he has interviewed some of the most successful entrepreneurs and celebrities in the world, and he always asks them how much they sleep. Just about every single one gets 8, even 9 hours a night. You do not have to sleep less in order to take advantage of more hours in the day. No, you sleep as much as you need, so that you wake up fully recharged, so that you can function at 100% during the hours you are awake, so treat your evening book-end with as much care and focus as you do the morning book-end.

Time-Blocking

Time blocking is just a way of scheduling your week so that you know what you're going to work on, and when. This is how you start to create flexibility and freedom for yourself within the week.

For example, at least Monday through Friday, make sure you're clear on when you want to wake up. If you want to wake up at 7am, then work your way backwards to figure out how much sleep you want to get. If you want to get 8 hours of sleep and you want to wake up at 7 that means you need to be asleep — not just in bed — by 11pm each night. If you need to be asleep by 11pm, that means you need about 45 minutes to wind down, so set a bed-time reminder alarm for 10. At that alarm, turn off all electronics, put everything away, finalize your brain dump. That will take about 15 minutes, and then you've got half an hour just to spend time with your partner, reading a good book or taking a bath and just relaxing so your brain can slow down before you go to sleep.

So that's the foundation of your time blocking. The next thing you put into the calendar is your time for self-care and family time. Schedule when you're going to do your self-care — your journaling, meditation, workouts, walks and so on. Then put in when you're going to be spending time with your family and your time off. Scheduling your time off is how you create freedom. If it's in the calendar, you will take it, because when you get to the end of the day, and the next task in your calendar is STOP, then you will. Everything you've scheduled for the day is done, and you can feel confident letting that be enough. If it's in the calendar, you actually do it, which is pretty amazing. Only once your self-care, family time and rest time are scheduled should you move on to scheduling those most important work tasks.

For example, when I was at Cisco, the most important tasks were client visits. I would look at the week ahead and schedule when I would be on site with clients, and then from that I would be able to schedule time to get all the administrative work done. I scheduled checking email twice a day. I would check in the morning, around 9am, and once more around 4pm before I finished up for the day at 5pm. People were amazed that I would only check my email twice a day, even though I was in the corporate world. They were like, "What do you mean, I'm checking my email all day long". I was too busy to check my email all day long. Email is just a long list of other people's priorities, but that doesn't make it my priority. I know what I need to do to get results, and I'll get to email once all the more important stuff is done.

These days I only check my email once a day, when my calendar says so. If you're a starting entrepreneur, there's certain tasks that you know are paramount — lead generation, sales calls, marketing — schedule all that first, and then figure out how to fit in the other things around it.

It all comes back to properly weighing what's important, and the only way that you can properly weigh what's important is by having clarity. The clarity of the ideal life you want to have, and again, it's not just about the business, it's not just about your career, but it's what would be ideal in every different part of your life.

There's an element of experimentation about what kind of time blocking is going to work for you. To begin with, you just have to implement something, and then, using the Review and Reflect cycle, you'll figure out what works and what doesn't. For me, I love what I do. I love working. And I will always love working way more than Maddy does. I'm a very strong masculine energy. For me, this work is my purpose, my passion, my mission, and it's very closely tied to my heart, my soul, my life. If someone were to tell me, "Zander, you can never work at all on weekends," I'd say, "Get out of my life, you do not belong here."

I tried fully taking every weekend off. But after a day and a half, I need a little bit of it back. It's not anxiety — I sincerely miss it. I miss helping my team grow. I miss inspiring them. I miss talking to clients. So I'm completely off from Friday afternoon at about 4pm, all the way through Saturday until Sunday morning. On Sunday morning, I time-block about two to three hours of working and planning and playing around with the business, and then I take the rest of Sunday off too. Maddy and I experimented a lot to figure out what really works for both of us. Her routine is different to mine: she's totally off from about midday on Friday, through all of Saturday and Sunday. During the week, she takes a 60 to 90 minute break in the middle of the day, where she makes sure to do nothing 'productive'. She just goes and hangs out at the beach, or she goes and gets some sun or reads a good book. That's what really works for her, as it allows her to recharge in her own way. She starts working early too, then takes her midday break, then clocks off about 5pm too.

You have to experiment with what works for you. It's very easy to let other people's routines and energy influence you, but working on someone else's schedule is eventually going to stress you out. Experiment, review, reflect and adapt.

TWELVE
SALES AND LEADERSHIP

"If your actions inspire others to dream more, learn more, do more and become more, you are a leader."

JOHN QUINCY ADAMS

What does it mean to be a leader?

Leaders go first. They pave the way. They set the vision, they take courageous action, they have faith, they inspire followers and impact others. Sounds like a lot of the qualities we've been trying to cultivate doesn't it?

In order to be successful, you must be a leader. So what does it take to be a great leader? It's actually easier than you think.

Sales and Leadership Are The Same Thing

What's your preconceived connotation of sales? Is it positive or negative?

How about leadership? Positive or negative?

Most people have negative connotations around selling and salespeople. On the other hand, the connotation around leadership is generally much more positive. In reality, neither are positive or negative. They're both just tools. Both sales and leadership are all about persuasion and influence. John Maxwell says that leadership is influence, and really, the same goes for sales. Both skillsets are about whether you can influence somebody else to make a decision, and take action.

What makes them positive or negative is how you use them. You can use both sales and leadership for good, or you can use sales and leadership for bad. One of my favorite salespeople of the last century was Martin Luther King. He sold an entire generation on a new idea, a new way of acting and behaving and thinking of what is possible. One of the most effective leaders of the last century was Hitler. He was a terrible person, and so his leadership took an entire country to a horrifying place and nearly plunged the whole world into darkness.

John Maxwell also says that the ability to lead determines a person's level of overall effectiveness. In your personal life and in your business, your ability to lead yourself, your ability to lead others, and your ability to lead other leaders will dictate your level of potential in this life. Period, end of statement. If leadership is that limiting factor, and leadership and sales are the same thing, then what I'm saying here is leadership and sales are paramount to any form of success.

No matter which of the Five Spokes of your life that you're looking at, without sales and leadership — without the ability to influence — you will never accomplish the things you want to accomplish, and so learning the fundamentals of these skills is one of the most important skills we can focus on.

The first step is to learn to lead yourself. You can't lead yourself without taking full ownership and influencing your thoughts, habits, actions and environments. See? It all comes back to influence. Once you take full ownership of your own outcomes, you can start to lead other people, and like I said earlier, the reason that leadership is so important is because whatever you want to accomplish in this life will include other people.

We've been selling since we were two years old. If you're a two-year-old and you want a cookie, you're selling your mom on giving you that cookie. You're asking, "Hey, can I have the cookie? Can I have a cookie? Can I have the cookie? Why not? Why not?" That's an early attempt at sales — you're trying to influence your mom to give you the cookie.

When you meet a cute girl or guy at the bar, you're selling that person on why they should have a conversation with you. You're trying to influence them into liking you so that you can build a relationship with them. When you spot a job that you want, you're selling yourself to get that career opportunity. When you ask someone to marry you, you're selling them on spending the rest of their life with you. All this is a form of sales, and as you can see, selling is really about whether you can get someone to take action with you. The 'sale' might happen over months or years as your cumulative behavior influences them towards a particular outcome. No matter how you look at it, anything that you ever do in life will require other people. If you want to have any form of satisfied relationships, if you want to have any form of impact on the world, if you want to have fulfillment in your life, the ability to influence and lead others is absolutely paramount.

When I quit my job to start an entrepreneurial business

there were a lot of risks. To other people's way of thinking, I was taking a huge risk throwing away a quarter of a million-dollar job to go after this. But I believed there was no way I could lose. I knew I wasn't going to quit. I knew I wasn't going to die. I knew I was gonna focus on growing. I did not have confidence that I could make money, but I had confidence in my resolve to go figure it out. And that came from complete ownership and 100% commitment to the point where I would have done anything to make sure that I figured it out. That's what it means to lead and influence yourself first. You have to have a deep belief in whatever you're selling or whatever you're doing. Because in the end, if you give yourself a back door, a way out, you're never going to make it. You have to be fully confident in selling yourself, in selling your products, your services, whatever they might be to actually be successful. If you don't believe in it, no one else will either.

The 7 Rules of Leadership

There are seven rules to leadership (and sales), and we're going to run through each of them in depth here. You can start applying them to yourself immediately, so that when the time comes to start leading others, you're ready. The seven roles of leadership and sales ... intention, lid, results, decision, belief, vision, reality.

1. INTENTION

John Maxwell says that "the measure of a leader is not the number of people who serve him, but the number of people he serves." The first rule is your intention: always lead with an intention to serve. Bring an intention to help others. Get rid of any self-serving intentions, any self-preserving intentions. That's really one of the most important differentiators here between any good leader or any good salesperson. People can sense when you have a good intention or when you don't. You can practically smell it. We talked about this back in the Execution section: don't be the sleazy, underhanded used car salesman that just wants to rip people off. Be their Yoda, their trusted advisor. Be someone they respect and want to follow. Let your intention be to serve the greater good.

2. THE LAW OF THE LID

The law of the lid comes from John as well. He says that your potential is only limited by your leadership capability: your 'lid', the upper limit of what your capabilities will allow. You will never be able to sell, influence, persuade or lead anybody above your current capability, and so your job is to make sure you're always pushing the lid a little higher.[1]

For example, if you are a 7 out of 10 leader, you will never lead or sell anybody who is above a 6. The people you will influence will mostly be 4s and 5s. The law of the lid states that if you show up as a 7, other people will show up as a 5 or 6. If you show up as a 10, other people will show up as an 8. And If you want people to show up as a 10, you have to show up as an 11.

My clients are top level entrepreneurs. If I want them to show up at a 10, and my team is coaching them, then my team has to show up at an 11. And because I lead my team so they can lead our clients, that means I have to show up at a 12. I can't be a 7 out of 10 leader and have a team that's a 9 or a 10 out of 10, leading clients above me. That'll never work. That's the law of the lid. You always have to be focusing on your own leadership capabilities, your own capacity, your character as a person first, so that you can lead at greater and greater heights.

3. RESULTS, NOT EXCUSES.

This one is simple: leaders get results. You either get results, or you can make excuses. You can't have both. A leader finds a way to get results. They get creative, they take brave action, they face their fears, they get results. In the end, leaders just win.

4. Decisions, confidently

Leaders don't just make decisions, they make decisions confidently, even in uncertainty. Confident decisiveness is a huge, huge part of whether or not people will follow you. So again, if you're confident to a level of 7 out of 10, other people will be confident to a 5 out of 10. When you make a decision, you have to have a 10 out of 10 confidence if you want other people to follow you. Not only do you have to make these uncertain decisions, you have to stand in them confidently.

When you make a decision, you are 100% committed to it. You fully commit to taking the action, doing the work, and following through. When you say you're going to do something, you do it. You can never be 100% confident of the results, but you can be 100% confident in your ability to do what's necessary.

5. Belief

Leaders are believers. If you want to build a skyscraper, you have to create the blueprints first. That's belief: it's creating the blueprints in your mind for what you're going to achieve, so that you can actually make it happen.

Leadership and sales are both just a transfer of belief. When two people interact, each one of them has their own beliefs. They have their own belief system and individual beliefs. And as the two people interact and their two belief systems collide, the stronger beliefs will absorb and replace the weaker beliefs.

If one person comes in and believes that a particular plan won't work, and someone else comes in who believes absolutely that the plan will work, in that interaction, one of these beliefs will consume the other, depending on whose belief is stronger. The one that wins out now contains the whole. I think of

Martin Luther King: he had this belief, this dream, of a world of equality, where people were not judged on their skin color. A lot of people did not believe that was possible. But he believed it so deeply that his belief spread like crazy. He believed it so deeply and so powerfully, that when he interacted with a small group, that group would absorb this belief, and it would become their own. And it would become so powerfully their own they could then go take it to more people. And it created this spread of the belief in equality and justice. This powerful belief, deeply seated with an intention of helping others, allowed it to spread far and wide. And that's the real power of belief. It can travel far beyond you, if you just believe enough.

6 AND 7: VISION AND REALITY

Your belief is built around a vision. And it's the power of this belief that brings your vision to reality — but a lot of people get stuck on the vision, and forget about the reality.

Obviously, you have to have a vision for where you want to go, the change that you want to see in the world. That's what people will start to align with and want to follow. But the role of the leader is to have one hand reaching for the stars, and the other hand firmly pulling the earth up behind you. In pursuing their vision, leaders are pulling earth toward the heavens. This is stressful. It is tenuous to reach and to pull at the same time. But too many would-be leaders forget about pulling reality along with them and get lost in the vision. Remember we talked about building momentum earlier? This is the same thing over again. It's easy to get momentum if you unhook the engine from the heavy payload on the rest of the train, but the payload is the point, and you need to get the engine and the train moving if you're going to end up anywhere meaningful. Good leaders have one hand reaching to the vision and the other hand firmly pulling reality along behind them.

Soft Front, Firm Back

Over the last several years I have worked with hundreds of coaches who in turn have gone on to lead thousands of clients of their own — and one thing I learned is that sales and leadership are really just another form of coaching.

To make it even simpler you can draw a connection to parenting as well. I like the parenting analogy here, because most of us have some exposure to different parenting styles, which makes this 'soft front, firm back' idea a bit easier to understand. We teach our clients that there are three types of parents (or coaches, or leaders).

There's the parent we call a jellyfish. They're complete pushovers — there's no backbone, their kids can just walk all over them and do whatever they want. Those parents tend to end up with little shits for kids. You see them out in public, and you think, "That child is a menace, *please* do something to redirect that." Being too soft is not a good thing as a parent, and nor is it a good thing as a coach or leader.

Then there's the hard-ass parent. They are like a brick wall — an immovable object that is cold, rigid and strict. These parents tend to end up with kids who feel unworthy and unloved. Their kids feel like they were never good enough for Mom or Dad's approval, and it creates a lot of self-worth issues. That style is not good either.

What you're really looking for is a balance between those extremes: a soft front paired with a firm back. These parents love on their kids, show them care and support, but also have the resolve to tell their kids when it's time to get to work or straighten up. These parents tend to end up with confident, secure kids who know that they're loved, that their parents will not allow them to fall too far, but who also understand boundaries and responsibility. This is also the kind of leader we strive to create at High Impact Coaching.

It's a beautiful balance between the soft front and firm back. It's about showing love, but also being willing to have difficult conversations. It's about having high standards for yourself and others, while providing the support and environment that makes those high standards attainable.

And of course, whatever applies to leadership also applies to sales. People don't care how much you know until they know how much you care. So you have to care. You have to really understand people, you have to be able to empathize with them, and connect deeply with them if they are going to trust you enough to follow you. People will only get out of their comfort zone as far as they feel supported. If you want to lead them to places that will take them outside of their comfort zone, they have to feel immensely loved and supported to be able to do it. That's what a soft front and firm back will allow you to do.

This supportive, empathetic style of leadership does not come naturally to everyone, but fortunately, it's a skill that can be developed just like any other. If you're having trouble empathizing, take ownership of that, and go build that muscle. How do you do that? Well, you go find a different perspective. Travel to some place that's completely different from what you know. Go look at how other people live, go hear how other people think and feel and function.

I had this hammered into me from a young age. One day when I was about three years old, my sister came home from school and made a negative comment about a Hispanic classmate. Next thing I knew, my parents were relocating us from San Diego to Tijuana, Mexico, where we would stay for the next six months. Talk about a change in perspective.

Sure, we were only little kids, but we saw a totally different way of living: no running water, no electricity. I saw the immense amount of care and love and connection that held the community together, how well they took care of each other. We continued to spend a few days down in Baja every few months for years after that, to remind us that for all the differences in our circumstances, we're all the same.

While I was working on this book, I interviewed my buddy Chris Vasquez, who had just been in Ghana for two months, helping to build infrastructure. He commented, too, that going somewhere with a completely different perspective makes you realize that we all want love and safety and a sense of meaning. And when you understand that, empathy naturally follows, and helps you understand how you can connect with your people and lead them in a way that is going to help them attain those universal desires.

Another key component here is communication and curiosity. To make sure that your people actually experience your 'soft front firm back' approach, you have to be willing to actively communicate. I'm always curious about my team members. I'm always asking questions about them, both about how things are going in their work, and also in their personal life. We have really open, honest communication. We call it radical candor. I tell my team members that there is nothing they can't tell me, nothing they shouldn't tell me, and that I will never hold anything they tell me against them. They could tell me I'm a terrible leader, they could tell me I'm running the business all wrong, they could tell me something I'm doing absolutely sucks, and I will hear it all gladly. It's all feedback for me — I can't fix something if I'm not aware that it's a problem.

This is called radical candor. Anybody in my organization can book a one-on-one with me. If they want to tell me something, they want to give me feedback, my door is always open. Each week we send out an email with all of our numbers, what we're working towards, and we wrap up with a link where team members can suggest one thing they think the business (and I) should stop, start, or continue to do more of. Then we take that feedback to the executive team meeting, and we vote on it all. Everybody has a say in what the business does.

We also do vision setting with everybody on the team. My mentor Jack Canfield once told me that your goal as a leader is for your vision to encompass the vision of everybody else on your team. The true strength of a leader is whether your vision can help everybody else under you accomplish their own vision.

Jim Rohn says that if you help enough people accomplish their dreams, inevitably, you will accomplish yours, and that's really the way I look at leading my team. I know the one-year, three-year and five-year goals of everybody on my team (and if they don't have the longer-term goals figured out, we keep working together to create them). Then we help break those goals down into tasks each person can accomplish over the next 30, 60 or 90 days. We're not just talking about career goals or income goals: we're talking about health goals, relationship goals, everything. My team members are my most important clients. I take care of my team more than I take care of anybody else because my team takes that care out to our clients. And it works: I have a team of mostly millennials, and in five years, only one person has ever left the team. What business can get 20 millennials to stick around for five years?!

5 Steps To Sell Anything

Now that we know the high level principles of what it takes to lead and influence others, let's get some strategies to drive it home. My clients and I have used these strategies to sell high-ticket coaching programs anywhere from $2000 up to

$100,000. I've also used this in the tech and SaaS industry, selling technology systems and networks for $30 million. The same process that I used to sell a $15,000 coaching package to a new client in a single conversation in a coffee shop also resulted in Disney purchasing a $27 million network from me while I was working at Cisco. Same process, just different details. These five steps will teach you how to sell anything.

Now, remember that these steps are the theory, not the tactics. Each industry has its own specific tactics, and you need to figure out the specifics for your industry. But when you combine those tactics with this framework, your sales conversations are going to work.

1. Intention

Everybody always thinks rapport is the first step in any sales process. It's not. The first step in any sales process actually happens before you even have any form of human interaction. It's about the true intention that you come into that interaction with, and this is the difference between being perceived as a salesperson and being a trusted adviser. See the similarities between sales and leadership?

This was something I learned at Cisco and I've carried it with me throughout the rest of my sales career. Coming into the conversation with the intention of supporting, understanding and empowering your client will help them to trust you, often more than they trust themselves: remember, we want to be Yoda to everyone around us. Is Yoda always nice? No. Does Yoda always tell you what you want to hear? No. But he'll tell you what you *need* to hear, and he'll keep your best interests in mind, even when it means pushing you to make scary decisions.

2. Connection

When you've set your intention straight, then you can focus on establishing a connection and building rapport. This is where the conversation becomes a bit like a game of catch: you throw the ball, they have to catch it. They throw it back to you, you have to catch it. Communicating is just about going back and forth so that it feels like there's a two-way connection there. This is super easy for some people, and really difficult for others. But having a true connection, having true rapport and the trust that comes with it is absolutely crucial. People don't normally buy from people that they don't know love and trust. There is the rare occasion, maybe around 2% of the time, that the problem is so severe and the solution is so needed that they will buy from anyone, but as a rule, that trust has absolutely got to be there.

If establishing this kind of connection is difficult for you, practice. Talk to people more and really pay attention to what they like and want. Read *Emotional Intelligence* 2.0. Really though, it's about learning to fully engage with the person in front of you. Stop thinking about yourself and start thinking about the other person. As soon as you do this, it becomes a lot easier to connect with people. Most of us are internalized and anxious because we're focused inward. As soon as we turn outward, we start to focus on this other person, trying to understand them, trying to figure out where they're coming from, why they do what they do. Turn your focus from yourself to them and you'll stop feeling nervous, you'll stop feeling anxiety, you'll stop feeling any form of stress. You'll just start to be curious. If you can just become curious about the other person, be interested in the other person, it's probably the quickest way to start to connect.

You don't need to be an *interesting* person, you need to be an *interested* person.

3. Problem Clarity

My head sales guy at High Impact Coaching, Cathal, used to own multiple karate studios. One day a very fit guy walked into one of the studios and asked a junior salesman if they did sparring classes. And the sales guy launched directly into pitching their sparring options, on and on and on. Cathal walks up and pauses his junior guy, and then asks their guest if he's actually looking for sparring. Turns out the answer was no. He actively did not want sparring, and was looking for gyms with a different focus. The junior sales guy was pitching sparring, because he assumed that's what this big guy wanted.

You have to get super clear on what your customer's problem really is before you start offering them solutions. Do not assume that you already know.

To do this, again, you have to get really comfortable interacting with people. You have to have really in-depth conversations where you can ask all kinds of questions and really get at the root cause of the issue, not just the surface-level symptoms. Think of a doctor trying to figure out why you are having pain in your abdominal region. They are going to dig deep and ask a ton of questions to get crystal clear on what's going on and how it happened:

- "What have you been eating recently?"
- "Have you had any physical trauma to the area?"
- "On a scale of 1-10, what's your stress level like?
- "How's your sleep?"

Don't be afraid to ask deeper, harder questions if you don't think you've got to the root cause — even if it takes multiple conversations over a long period of time. And remember that sales is a human process. In the end, there's a decision maker, or a couple of decision makers, and the decision almost always gets made on emotion, not necessarily logic. It is a combination of both, and so you need to get comfortable asking the questions that will give you a clear picture of what that decision-maker needs both logically and emotionally in order to move forward.

4. QUALIFICATION

Once you're clear on someone's problem, most people want to go straight into pitching a solution. But if you do that, you skip one of the most important steps in sales: qualification.

If I'm going to pitch my solution, and I want to show confidence in my solution, I need to make sure that everybody in the conversation is on the same page as me.

Once I know the problem back to front, and it's time to propose a solution, I am going to get super clear with the client about what it will take to make the solution work. For example, if I was pitching a network to Disney, I couldn't promise it would work unless I had certain agreements from them: "I would need unvetted access to your team, my team would need this and that information, I'd need a weekly meeting with your team to make sure everything is on track during the implementation, and I'll want a one-on-one with you personally to make sure everything is going to plan. Is this something you guys would be able to provide?"

This is the qualification. You ask them to confirm that they are actually going to be able to meet you at the high level you're going to provide. Qualification is so key: you're interviewing your potential audience. If you're going to be coaching someone one-on-one, or providing any kind of product or service, there are two parties in that relationship. You could provide the best service in the world, but if they're not going to do the work, it'll never work. You have to make sure that they are on the same page as you, and that they're willing to do the work.

There are some key questions I ask to make sure each new client is fully on board with what's going to happen when we work together. Number one: "Are you willing to be decisive and take action outside of your comfort zone? This is going to push you outside of your comfort zone and your life will change." That's scary for a lot of people, even though it will change for the better.

Number two: "Are you willing to be coachable? What you're doing right now has not gotten you where you want to be, and I'm going to be telling you things you probably don't want to hear. But the feedback you don't want to hear is probably the feedback you need to hear the most. Are you willing to take that feedback with an open mind?"

Number three" Are you willing to do it for the right reasons? I don't like working with people that are only in it for the money, rather than for the impact."

If they can legitimately answer yes to all those questions, I will let them know that I'm confident that I can help them get to where they want to be". Without that agreement, I cannot confidently say I can get them there. That agreement is a really important part of the sales process for two reasons. It obviously prepares them for a great working relationship, and secondly, it makes them see that you're honest. You're not trying to promise whatever it takes just to get the sale. It's very 'unsalesy', because it's the truth. You're telling people the truth about what it's going to take, and helping them come to a mutual understanding and agreement about how it might work to get there. I'm a big fan of the "under-promise, over-deliver" approach to client care. I will under-promise on what I tell them we can achieve up front, so that I can guarantee we over-deliver, above and beyond their expectations, in the actual execution.

5. PITCHING

Everybody thinks that pitching is the most important piece to selling, but it's only a small final detail to close out the rest of the process. Only after you've established a good intention, you've really connected with someone, you've gotten problem clarity *and* you've qualified the client should you go anywhere near pitching.

Pitching always makes people squirm a little bit, because this is when you start talking about the money. Remember — money is just a placeholder for value. Frankly, the easiest way to help get comfortable with having this conversation is to practice. Detach from it. Practice in front of a mirror to the point where the phrases have no emotional bearing on you. The numbers are just numbers, and remember that talking about the actual specifics of the money should really be a minimal part. Focus much more on the value you're providing. Focus on the benefits of what you're doing, how it solves their specific problem, what they can expect from this whole process. When you focus on the value, the whole conversation changes. It ceases to be about the money and entirely about what's going to change in their world.

Let's take health and wellness coaching as an example. I always tell people weight loss is probably the most valuable coaching business in the world. But people don't believe me. Why? Because Weight Watchers charges $30 a month, Jenny Craig charges $30 a month, but they don't get results. There's so many people that go through those programs and don't get permanent results. They yo-yo diet — maybe they lose some weight to begin with, but then they go right back up to where they were. For somebody who's been 30, 40, 50 pounds over-weight for 10, 15, 20 years, how is that affecting them? They can't be there for their kids like they want to be. It's causing all kinds of problems in their marriage. They're worried about a chronic illness, or that they might die decades before their time. And they're not living their life. They're living in pain and struggling all day long. So what would meaningful, permanent weight loss mean to that person? What would it be worth to never have to struggle again, to always have the energy they wanted, to re-engage with their family, to get their life back? What is 30 years of life actually worth? When you start to explain that to people, it's no wonder the lightbulb goes on: we have about 35 coaches who are all able to sell weight loss for $4000, $5000, $8000 for two to three month programs. Because when it comes to your pitch, you're comparing the *value* to the cost. Everybody gets caught up in the cost side of it, but in reality, your price is dictated by the value that you bring someone.

Mastering these five steps is different in every industry, but practice is key. Whether you are selling $30 million networks with a 12-month timeline, or $15,000 coaching programs in a 45-min interaction at a coffee shop, you will have different specific tactics and scripts, but when you get this flow down it'll benefit everything in your life — from your business to getting your kids to eat healthier foods and brush their teeth.

Problem, Agitate, Solve

Another form of sales is what is referred to as copywriting. You can think of copywriting as sales in written form, and I am about to teach you one of the most powerful frameworks ever invented to influence people with the written word.

Dan Kennedy, one of the greatest marketers of all time once said that if everybody just communicated with the PAS (Problem, Agitate, Solve) framework, they would achieve all their goals in life. It's a framework to communicate, to persuade and influence. You start by talking about the problem. You agitate the emotions that the problem is causing and what it's costing. Then you solve it with your offering. It's so simple.

If you go look at any good TED Talk, I can just about guarantee the talk is structured in the PAS framework. The speaker starts with the problem, agitates what it's really costing people, and then explains the solution at a high level. That's literally all it is. You can use this framework to sell anything, and you can use this to persuade people to take action.

The biggest problem I see in the coaching space is that so many coaches are so passionate about what they do. They're experts at what they do as a coach. They've spent months, maybe even years becoming an expert in that space, whether it's health and wellness, relationships, life coaching, transformational coaching, and they're so good at it. But they can't make money. Because to build a coaching business, you need expertise in two things: coaching and business. They've got the coaching side down, but nobody ever taught them how to do business. Nobody ever taught them how to connect and engage with clients. Nobody taught them how to communicate in order to get consistent leads, or how to enroll clients at the prices they really deserve.

Because of this, so many coaches are afraid of the business side of things. They may spend months, even years working on their business until eventually it turns into a grind. 95% of coaches will never make it full time. 19 out of 20 coaches will never make it full-time, and according to Glassdoor, the ones who do will only average an income of $46,000 per year. That's just not worth it, and it doesn't have to be this way.

If you learn how to connect with your audience and generate leads consistently, if you learn how to price your programs in a way that gets you the profit and the income you deserve, and you learn how to deliver in a way that gets referrals and clients coming back to you over and over again, you'll never have to worry about scaling the business. You'll never have to worry about going back to a 9-to-5. You can have a six-figure or multiple six-figure coaching business that can scale well into the future.

And if you didn't catch it, the last three paragraphs were an example of the PAS framework.

---

1. *John C. Maxwell*, July 19 2013, "The Law of the Lid", by John C. Maxwell.
   https://www.johnmaxwell.com/blog/the-law-of-the-lid/

THIRTEEN
AIRPLANE MODE

"Believing stress is bad for you is the 15th largest cause
of death in the US"

STANFORD PSYCHOLOGIST, KELLY
MCGONIGAL

Now that you know how to manage your time, how to lead and
how to sell, it's time to learn how to manage yourself, both
mentally and physically. Creating your dream life is hard work.
I'm not going to lie to you: there will be days that feel extremely
stressful. There will be days that make you wonder if it's all
worth it. It absolutely is — there's nothing that can beat living
life on your own terms. But to make sure we don't get overwhelmed by the hard days, there are some key things to understand about stress and recharging.

Your Stress Cup

Imagine that in your body there is a cup, and all your physiological stress goes into this cup, and it doesn't matter what kind of stress we're talking about here — it all goes in together. For example, if I'm training for a triathlon, the physical stress of that goes into the cup. At the same time, I'm running an entrepreneurial business, and the pressure I feel from that also goes into the cup. The stress from any issues I'm having in a relationship go into that cup, the strain on my body from a bad night of sleep — all that goes into this one cup. Of course, there's not an actual cup somewhere in your body, but it demonstrates the fact that your body only has one system for managing all your different types of stress. Whether it's good stress (like you get from working out) or bad stress (like you get from having a fight with someone), your body really can't tell the difference, and so your job is to stop that system from getting overloaded.

I notice this a lot with the strength and fitness coaches we work with. They'll be doing high-intensity workouts that put a lot of pressure on their bodies, and they don't realize that the high amounts of stress they're feeling in their daily lives is actually being exacerbated by that exercise. One small thing will happen in the business and they'll freak out, because their cup is full to the brim — they're pushing themselves hard in the gym, hauling ass to make their business work, and sometimes neglecting the rest and relationships that would help them empty out that stress cup a bit.

The goal here is to stop your cup from getting too close to full. When it gets too full, one little thing can make the whole thing overflow, which can take you out for days, weeks, or even longer.

That's why there's a whole chapter on stress in this section.

Stress is one of the biggest reasons people don't do what they need to do. It's one of the most powerful excuses we give ourselves. We've talked a lot about taking 100% ownership — and this goes for your stress and anxiety too. You can use stress and anxiety as an excuse to avoid doing what you need to do, or you can take ownership of it, put strategies in place to keep that cup at a manageable level, and keep on keeping on towards your dreams. And I'm not talking about masking your stress and anxiety with a pill. You can cure stress and anxiety with tools and strategies that give you back control and allow you to overcome those challenges from the inside out, and we'll talk more about those strategies towards the end of this chapter.

Stress vs Worry

Stress gets a bad rap. But, as with most things, whether stress is good or bad is completely contextual.

The body and mind require stress to grow (this type of positive stress is known as eustress). The physiological stress of working out, for example, is what allows us to develop lean muscle mass, burn more fat, and release the neurochemicals that make us feel rewarded. It's the same when you're learning something new and challenging: the stress on your brain leads to the formation of new neural pathways, strengthened memory and greater neural activity. All good things, right? That kind of pressure also triggers the release of dopamine and norepinephrine in our brain, the combination of which creates the feeling of motivation. Without stress, you don't grow. You don't get better. We all know that too much pressure can cause anxiety and burnout, (this type of negative stress is called distress). But too little pressure can cause depression and stagnation. What we want here is a happy medium; let's stay away from those two extremes as much as possible.

Stanford professor Kelly McGonigal says that the effect of stress is all about how you perceive it: "Once you appreciate that going through stress makes you better at it, it can be easier to face each new challenge."[1] McGonigal and her associate Alia Crum found that viewing stress as a helpful part of life leads to better health, better emotional wellbeing, and better productivity. But when you view stress as a purely negative part of life, it leads to worse health, more procrastination and increased reliance on harmful coping mechanisms (like drinking too much or picking fights with people).

McGonigal spent ten years teaching that stress took years off of your life. Then in her TED talk in 2013, she revealed new data that completely changed her mind.[2]

An eight-year study in the US with 30,000 participants found that people who suffered from high-stress lives and believed stress was bad for you had a 43% increased chance of death compared to people in the cohort who also had high stress, but believed that stress had no impact on their heath. In fact, the group who didn't believe stress was bad for them had the lowest chances of death of everybody in the study.

Think about how crazy that is for just a second: how you think about stress literally changes how your body responds to it. So embracing your body's stress response is more important than reducing stress.

In your business, in your relationships, eustress is beneficial for you, causes you to take action, motivates you, pushes you forward. Distress causes you to freeze or give up. And the difference between the two is all in perspective.

What we need to differentiate now is the difference between stress and worry. Worry is the fear-based story we replay over and over in our mind about a situation that has not even occurred yet. Worry adds distress to your stress cup, and quickly, so next time you notice yourself getting worried, or telling yourself that you feel really stressed out, take a quick step back. Is it stress, or is it worry? If it is stress, is it distress or could it be eustress? If it's distress, how can you find a way to rework the situation so it becomes eustress? If you tell yourself that stress is a bad thing, then every time you get pushed, you're going to think, "I need to go sit on the couch and watch some Netflix and relax." But if you tell yourself stress is a good thing, then anytime you get pushed, you're going to get into action. Embrace your body's stress response — it's preparing you to rise to this challenge and to be courageous.

The Need For Control

Remember earlier in the book we talked about the Serenity Prayer? Here it is again to jog your memory:

"God grant me the serenity to accept the things I cannot change, courage to change the things I can, and the wisdom to know the difference."

A lot of worry and anxiety comes from a desire for control. You've set your goals and your vision, and you've created a clear desire for the end state you're working towards. But the only thing that's truly within your control is the process. The outcome is not within your control. You can do everything within your power to make something happen and still not get the result you wanted. You can control the process, you can control the input, but you can never control the output, because we are acting within an environment where other actors are adding their own inputs into this situation, which can suddenly shift your outcome in a different direction. It's important to remember that. If you don't get the outcome you want, don't torture yourself thinking, "I should have done this or that." Let it go. You can't change it now. Don't create the dissonance and frustration for yourself — accept reality as it is and move forward.

Next time, do everything you can to control the inputs. Put your best effort into the process, adding what you've learned along the way. And then let go of the outcome. It's scary to learn to surrender the result, but it's not within your control. If you can do this, you will always be fulfilled. You will always be able to let go of worry, because you did everything you could by focusing on the process. As soon as you accept the reality of where you are, you can start to make changes and move forward.

I learned this the hard way about a month after I quit my job. I had hired a mentor to help me figure out what to focus on, and he asked me to build a landing page to start collecting emails. I had never built a landing page before, and I had no idea what I was doing. But I'm a fast learner, and I was pretty confident in my capabilities, so I went off and figured out how to build a landing page, and shared it with my mentor a few days later. Now, I knew this thing wasn't going to be a home run. I knew it wouldn't be a 10 out of 10, but I thought it would be, like, a 5 out of 10. He took one look at it and said, "This is worthless." My stomach dropped through the floor. I forced myself to ask him for a score out of 10. "Negative 1. We need to completely start over, this will never work."

I was livid. For the next two days I was convinced I should just stop working with him. *Negative 1? Me?!* Eventually I calmed down though, and realized that at that moment, I was not good enough. It made me want to scream, but I had to accept that even though I'd expected to be at a 5 out of 10, I was at a negative 1. I spent some time digesting that, and then I went all the way back to the beginning. I accepted that to get to a 10 out of 10 from a negative 1, I was going to have to do a whole lot of work, and I got to it. The weird thing was that I started to excel much faster than I thought I would — and it's because I had accepted how much work it was going to take to get where I wanted to be. Accepting an outcome I hated allowed me to take control of the future process and change the next outcome. Not only will relinquishing your need to control help you make progress faster, it will also help you keep your stress cup under control.

Stress Relieving Tools

There are four tools that I use extensively to manage my own stress, and all the most successful entrepreneurs I know use some combination of these themselves. These are meditation, cold therapy, fear journaling and breath work. There are decades worth of data on all of them for their positive effect on stress and wellbeing, and I can honestly say I would not have the level of success I have today without them. Remember that the goal is not to get rid of stress. You need stress to grow. So if you want to grow faster, the goal should be to implement the tools that allow you to empty your stress cup faster and make it bigger so you can handle more.

1. MEDITATION

If you're not meditating, that's your choice. I don't think it's the right choice, but it's your life. There's so much science behind the benefits of meditating that it's not even a question anymore. Choosing not to do it is like choosing not to work out, or choosing not to sleep. Meditation will keep you healthier, it'll help you live longer, you'll be happier, you'll be a better communicator, you'll have less anxiety.

I started out with the Headspace app, just doing 10 minutes a day. Even that small start was really beneficial. I eventually got into Vedic meditation, and I've been doing that for the last four years now. It's similar to transcendental meditation. I do 20 minutes, twice a day, and it's like an industrial-strength stress release. I probably wouldn't have survived starting my own business without it, because there was so much psychological and physiological demand on me that I wouldn't have been able to handle otherwise.

There are many different forms of meditation. If you're just making a start, download the Headspace app or the Calm app, and start with 10 minutes a day. Once you've established a habit, you can start trying other types of meditation, like transcendental or Vedic, to figure out what works for you, and scale it up from there as you need it.

2. Cold Therapy

This is basically jumping into a cold plunge pool, getting under a cold shower, or going for a swim in icy water. Immersing your body in cold water basically supercharges your immune system, triggers thermogenesis and cell regeneration, and has the added benefit of training your brain to become tougher. It causes a crazy cascade of hormones through your body that make you extremely focused and motivated, and will keep your energy stable for hours afterwards. And if you do it before going to bed, it will do the opposite, getting rid of all the energy hormones, and you will sleep like a baby.

I have a cold plunge at my house now. I take my shower in the morning, then jump straight in the cold plunge before I head to my desk to start the day. Now, you don't have to start at that level. Get into your normal hot shower, enjoy that. Then at the end of your shower, turn it to the coldest possible setting and do it for 30 seconds. Gradually increase it to a minute or two — as long as you can take it. I normally just sit there and count through 10 deep breaths of 10 seconds. That normally puts me somewhere between a minute to a minute and a half and then I get the hell outta there. I hate it, but I also love it so much. I don't need coffee to start my day anymore because it makes me feel so energized.

3. BREATH WORK

I recently had Tyler Forbes, founder of Breathe Degrees and a leading breathwork expert on my podcast, and he said we're never really taught how to breathe, which is a weird thought, but that this is actually super important, because your breath can dictate your state. Fast, deep breaths through the mouth can excite your state. It shifts you into that high-alert, fight or flight state, where your sympathetic nervous system is in control. This is great if you're about to do some sprints or before you do a heavy set at the gym — you'll feel like you just got a shot of adrenaline.

But if you breathe in and out slowly through your nose, it shifts your body to the parasympathetic nervous system, also known as the state of 'rest and digest'. It calms you right down. So if you're feeling distressed or worried, focus on your breathing. Do 10 big deep breaths, in and out through your nose. Repeat as long as you need to. I do this a few times a day to reset my state and to make sure I'm in a calm space to work from. There are dozens of different types of breathwork exercises that you can find from practitioners like Tyler and Breathe Degrees that can range from helping you focus, to helping you destress to literally making you feel like you just took Ayahuasca and blasted off to another dimension (those ones are fun).

4. FEAR JOURNALING

Most people have heard of journaling, but as we talked about earlier, fear journaling is much more specific. I do it first thing in the morning to get any anxieties and fears out of my head, and I recommend all my clients do the same. 95% of our brain is subconscious, 5% is conscious, and all of our fears are marinating down in that subconscious. Most of us try to ignore our fears, because we're worried we'll bring them into reality if we think about them too much. But it's the opposite — if you leave them stewing down in your subconscious, that 95% is going to move you towards the fears, instead of away from them. You want to bring them to the forefront of your mind so you can feel through them, move through them and release them.

This might be one of the most powerful things I've ever done for stress relief, because you actually go sit in your anxieties, your fears and your worries. By actually acknowledging it all, you take the burden off your subconscious and shift those fears into the realm where you can actually think consciously and actively about them — instead of feeling like you're always at their mercy.

I literally just grab a journal and I will journal the most negative, dark, shitty stuff that I can think of. I write out all the fears, all the anxieties, all the worries. And as I sit in all that, it dissipates. What you resist persists. When you start to look directly at your fears, get up close and intimate with them, they stop being so scary. It's like turning on the lights in a dark room. Once you can see what's in there, you stop being afraid.

Do this for as long as you can each day. Start with 10 minutes. Don't try to turn it into something positive. This is not where you try to do counter-affirmations to your fears. Don't try to transform your fears into anything else. Just experience them. Go sit in the negative so you learn to actually move through those emotions. Just feel each fear until it's gone. On the other side of that, you will find motivation, you'll find inspiration.

This is how I processed AJ's death and was back to being able to fully function within five or six months. You never really get over something like that, but I was able to get moving again by actively searching for the grief and fear and pain every day. I sat with those feelings every day until they stopped hurting so much.

---

1. *Stanford News*, May 7 2015, "Embracing stress is more important than reducing stress, Stanford psychologist says", by Clifton B. Parker.
    https://news.stanford.edu/2015/05/07/stress-embrace-mcgonigal-050715/
2. TEDGlobale 2013, "How to Make Stress Your Friend", by Kelly McGonigal.
    https://www.ted.com/talks/
    kelly_mcgonigal_how_to_make_stress_your_friend?language=en#t-127972

FOURTEEN

FORD VS FERRARI, REVISITED

"Take care of your body. It's the only place you have to live."

JIM ROHN

If you want to have an optimal life, where you're making great money, you have all the freedom you want, you have great relationships — you need to make sure that you're not treating the Ferrari of a body that life has given you like a beat-up old Ford Pinto. Your body is one of the most powerful tools you will ever be given, but if you treat it like crap, it's going to work like crap and eventually it will just grind down until it breaks. But if you can look after your body, you're going to be able to perform at a level that most people can't even imagine.

Getting to peak performance is not about hustling harder than everybody else. Yes, you'll have to work hard to get the life you want, but there are so many misconceptions about this. It's not about working 80 hours a week, posting updates while you're pooping, emailing at all hours of the night. Performing at your peak is about being as productive as possible *while you're working*, and having clear boundaries around when you're not working, so that during those breaks, you're actually recharging so that you can come back and keep hitting it hard when it's time.

Slowing Down to Speed Up

I consider my body a battery. It's a good battery, it's got a long charge, but it's still a battery, and at some point, I need to recharge it.

Most people spend the majority of their time functioning in "low power mode." Think about how that goes on your phone: everything goes slower, some functions don't work, and you just start to get anxious that you're not going to be able to keep using it. So if your phone's on low power mode, what do you do? You put it on airplane mode, and you charge it. It charges faster on airplane mode because it's not pinging out a signal all the time.

It's the same with your body. You need to regularly find a way to get yourself on airplane mode, when you completely disconnect and turn off. Physiologically, our brains have not changed much over the last 50,000 years. But over the last 50 years, the amount of input and distraction has gone up exponentially. Our body and mind have not had time to adapt to that new level of stimulation, which is why we're seeing addictions and depression so closely linked to the amount of time we're spending on our devices.

Schedule regular time for a digital detox. It is really important to reset and just be present in real life, rather than absorbing everything second-hand through a screen. Saturday is normally my digital detox day. We'll turn off the internet, we'll turn off our phones, and spend the day just hanging out with friends, chilling on the beach or whatever we feel like, as long as we can just be present and avoid taking in a bunch of input.

And if you find yourself working seven days a week, stop. Even God took the seventh day to rest. And if that's not enough for you, so did David Goggins. Take at least one day per week completely off from working. Rest. You have to slow down to recharge, so that you can speed back up.

When I left Cisco, I realized the one thing more important to me than money was time. And as I became an entrepreneur, I realized the one thing more important than time was focus. I would rather work 40 hours a week and be 100% focused then work 80 hours a week and be 50% focused. I'll get significantly more done and better done if I work 40 hours a week, 100% focused, and the way I do that is by taking two 20-minutes breaks to meditate each day, I take Saturdays completely off, and once a quarter, I take one week completely off. I am a hard worker and have a consistently high output, and it's only because I take regular breaks that I'm able to do it.

Control Your Intake

When I was 7 years old I thought it would be funny to put mud into our neighbor's gas tank.

What do you think happened? (Well, besides the obvious — I got caught and grounded for three months for being a menace to society) Do you think the car ran well after that?

Absolutely not. They had to call a tow truck in and replace the whole gas tank and gas lines, and I learned an important lesson. Cars don't run well on mud.

Like I said before, your body is a Ferrari. If you have a

Ferrari and you pour mud into the gas tank, it's not going to function very well, even though it's one of the best designed machines out there. Instead, you would put the best gasoline money can buy in that bad boy, and you would make sure it had the oil and all the other inputs it needs to perform like it's meant to. It's the same with your body. Putting shitty food into your body is like pouring mud in the gas tank of that Ferrari. Your body is an incredible machine, so fuel it accordingly.

Figuring out the fuel that's right for you — the types of food that make you feel best and in what quantities — is going to be down to some experimentation. It varies a lot for different people, and I've done a lot of experimentation with different diets to find out what really works for me. I've tried the Paleo diet, I've gone vegan, I've tried all kinds of things, and now I know exactly what I need to eat in order to perform at my best every day. For me, that means eating about 90% plant-based foods, with the occasional piece of high-quality organic meat.

Now, all of this is not to say I don't occasionally eat shitty food or indulge myself with something I enjoy. I love eating out and having cool experiences with people, and I'm not going to be so rigid about my nutrition that I never have any fun. But I know that if 90% of the time, or even 80% of the time, I'm consuming good, minimally processed foods that are high in nutrition, that my body will be able to maintain itself and continue to function as I want it to. I have not gotten sick to the point where I cannot work for the last five years. I've gotten sniffles, I've felt under the weather, but I fuel my body in such a way that it runs like a perfectly oiled machine.

I take the same approach with coffee and alcohol. Both have a special place in our culture, and I think a lot of people use them more for the emotional scaffolding they provide than because they actually enjoy them. I drink decaf coffee, because I love regular coffee so much that when I drink it, I end up drinking way too much and bouncing off the walls — not optimal for my performance. I'll have an espresso if we're in Italy on vacation but for a work day? Decaf is just fine, and green tea or matcha on the days I want something else, but I will never drink coffee as a 'pick-me-up'. That's a signal that I haven't recharged right.

Same goes for consuming alcohol. I love a good tequila, but I'll save it for special occasions — say, Maddy and I go on a date night or we're travelling somewhere that makes amazing tequilas and we want to do a tasting. It's not a tool I use to wind down at the end of the day or as a habitual part of my week, because I know that any alcohol will mess with my focus and ability to perform the next day. Then I'll want coffee to prop myself up, and then more booze again later to slow myself down... and it just makes a crazy cycle that I don't want to get stuck in. Whenever I indulge, I just make sure that I'm paying attention to *why*. Why am I having this espresso? If the answer is: I'm on vacation, and I'm just relaxing and having a good time, and I love the taste of espresso — fine. But if the answer is that I'm tired and cranky and I need it to get going, that's no bueno. Again, same thing for alcohol. Why am I having this glass of tequila? I'm enjoying date night with Maddy. Fine. But if the answer is that I'm uncomfortable in a group of strangers at a party and I need a little social lubrication, or because I had a stressful day and need to take the edge off? Not good, and I need to find a healthier way to deal with those emotions.

Move Or Grow Roots

As a kid my dad used to tell me to get off the couch or I might get stuck to it. He'd also tell me to get moving on my chores before I grow roots.

So being naturally curious I always wondered if people could actually grow roots.

After about two hours of Googling a few years ago, I gratefully found out the answer was no. But I did find out you *could* actually get stuck to the couch. There are multiple stories of people staying in chairs or couches for months at a time and the fibers fusing to their skin!

First of all: WTF?!

And if that's not reason enough to not sit on the coach for too long, let's talk about the benefits of moving regularly (every hour or two, actually).

We all know theoretically that we need to exercise and move our bodies. But when you're on this journey of transforming your life, it's gotta go from being theoretical to being 100% practical, for several reasons. First up, moving your body helps you manage your stress cup. You don't need to be killing yourself every workout — you'll remember that very intense workouts can actually add stress — but moderate exercise releases a whole lot of feel-good hormones that reduce the sense of worry and pressure that can drag us down so much. Secondly, exercise moves lymph through your body, which is how your system flushes out toxins and delivers various nutrients to where they need to be. Unlike your circulatory system, the lymph is not driven by a pump like the heart — it needs you to move in order for it to keep flowing. The contractions of your muscles push the lymph around your body to filter all the nasties out.

It doesn't really matter what kind of movement you decide to do. And it doesn't have to take up hours every day. A 20-minute jog is great. So is lifting weights in the gym. I love rock climbing and running around on the beach with my dog. Maddy loves yoga and Pilates. Whatever it is you actually enjoy doing with your body, do it for 20 or 30 minutes every day. Sure — if you love intense workouts or you like a longer session, that's great too, but just make sure you're getting up and moving your body every day. You will have so much more energy, focus and clarity than you will by sitting in your chair for eight hours without a break. Believe me, getting your blood pumping and your lymph moving will give you far more productivity than the extra 20 or 30 minutes of staring at your screen.

Go. To. Sleep.

The most successful people in the world get the sleep they need. Some entrepreneurial gurus push this idea that you should be sleeping four hours a night so that you can work more, but it's bullshit. Unsustainable, dangerous bullshit. Did you know that it's now illegal all over the world in sleep studies to deprive people of sufficient sleep? Just a few weeks of three or four hours a night has such catastrophic health consequences that it's not ethically acceptable to do it to people. It's the same reason that sleep deprivation is used as a type of torture. Your body *must* sleep. Your brain *needs* sleep. Sleep is when crucial physiological processes occur — it's when all kinds of neuro-toxins are flushed from the brain, when cellular repair happens, when immunity is amplified, where trauma starts to be resolved, where memory is formed... you will never get the life you want if you don't get the sleep you need.

Leading sleep researcher Dr. Matthew Walker is very clear that for most people, eight hours is the ideal minimum per night. Some people need a bit more, some people need a bit less, but if you don't have a clear idea yet of how much you specifically need, start with eight hours and figure it out from there. If you're doing heavy workouts where you're trying to put on muscle mass, you will need more. If you're experiencing a lot of stress of any kind, you will probably need more. Yes, there will be times that you get less. Sometimes it will happen for days or even weeks in a row. But it's absolutely key that you keep a close handle on your sleep. It is the single most impactful factor on your performance. If you have a stretch where you're not getting enough sleep for whatever reason, figure out how to catch up. Take naps if you have to, get black-out blinds, supplement with magnesium or melatonin, cut out alcohol at night, try blue-light blockers (they knock me out) — do whatever it takes to make sure you get it under control, because it has a cascade effect onto your focus, your willpower, your consumption, your mood. When you get the right amount of sleep, not only will your focus be at 100% the next day, but you will actually be able to enjoy this life you're designing and live long enough to fully experience it.

FIFTEEN
MONEY MASTERY

"Money is a terrible master but an excellent servant."

P.T. BARNUM

Whether or not we want to admit it, money is probably the most influential factor in our world today. Money influences absolutely everybody and everything.

Money is a driver and a tool that is deeply connected to us on a psychological level.

If you look at Maslow's Hierarchy of Needs, money has a fundamental part to play at every level:

MASLOW'S HIERARCHY OF NEEDS

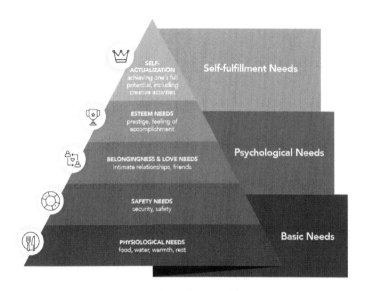

If you look at the very bottom layer, our physiological needs, money allows us to pay for food. It buys us time to rest and to maintain our physical bodies. At the next level, safety, money enables us to pay for somewhere to live, and allows us to pay for the basics that make us feel safe and secure. Having money beyond what we need to take care of ourselves also gives us status, and so on the level of love and belonging, money can make it easier to find a partner and to feel confident in building a life with them, including having children. It also gives us a sense of belonging, of being equals with our peers and community, which protects us from feeling shame and fear of exile.

Money can have a role to play in your self-esteem, too — if you know that you've worked hard for your money, and you're proud of how you look after it, that can have a positive impact on how you see yourself. And finally, money is an amazing tool when it comes to self-actualization: not only can you use money to pay for coaching and growth experiences, but you can also start to share your money in ways that have a positive impact far beyond your own life. Of course, we all know that money isn't what makes you happy. It will help, for sure — it's hard to be happy when you're broke — but we need to be clear about the role of money and how we can make it serve us, rather than getting stuck serving it.

Money Mindset

As I said earlier, money is just a physical or digital placeholder for social value. When I hire someone to do something for me, I either have to provide that person with a service or product of the same value, or I have to pay that person money to represent the value they are bringing me.

Money wasn't always cash like we know it today. Hundreds or thousands of years ago, if you wanted enough flour to make bread for a year, maybe you'd say, "Give me that flour and I'll give you this goat," or whatever a fair trade would have been back in the day. Eventually though, trading all these physical items got unwieldy, especially when you're looking at a level of trading between cities or countries. That's how physical money was invented: it's a placeholder of value that is much easier to measure and manage than the actual items being traded.

While I was working on this book, Maddy and I took a week-long trip to Costa Rica. I loved it, and so I will absolutely be buying more plane tickets to go there in the future. Now, I don't have a service that American Airlines wants. They don't want my coaching, so I can't trade them that service. So instead, I give them money whenever I want to fly down there, and in turn, they can use that money for things they actually want or need.

Once you start to understand that, money starts to have less of a hold on you. Your perception of money starts to change, drastically. If you want to make more money, this shift in perspective allows you to see that getting paid more simply means providing more value.

It's key to understand that money is not good or bad. We create all these stories around money, but ultimately it is just a tool, just a placeholder. If you're a good person, and you're doing good things, you're providing value in a good way to the world, then you should be making more money. And money will just make you more of who you are. It'll be a tool that'll expand the value that you're bringing. If you're a bad person, money can absolutely be used for bad, but I'm going to assume that since you're here, you're not a bad person and you're going to use your money to bring good into the world. The nature of money really depends on what you're doing with it and why.

The Money Pipeline

Money is meant to flow. It's meant to move. A lot of people try to store value — they hide their cash under bed, or leave it piling up in a savings account. They try to hold onto it. Everybody wants to make more money, but nobody loves spending money to get it. But that's the way it often works. Money is a lot like a pipeline: if you take a hose and you block one end, can any more water flow in? No. You have to let some water flow out for more to flow in, and money is the same: you have to allow money to go out for money to come in.

This is why it's so key to understand the difference between investing and spending. You don't just want to spend money without thinking about it: for your money pipeline to flow effectively, you want to make sure that the money going out will help you grow, help you increase your skills and will improve your financial situation. For example, coaching, training or great experiences will all help make your life better and help you keep growing. Buying a bigger TV or a whole new wardrobe every season will not.

I spend a lot of money, but every time I make a purchase, I ask myself: is this an investment or an expense? Is this thing going to help me grow, or is something that is going to depreciate in value and eventually disappear without changing anything about my life?

A good example is investing in yourself. Investing in yourself is probably one of the most important money decisions you will ever make. It's something you need to continue to do for the rest of your life, but a lot of people have issues around this. Why? Because they spent $100,000, getting a student loan that hasn't shown any return, so they're afraid of investing in themselves again, even though it would help them grow past that previous experience. You always need to be investing a large proportion of your income into yourself, because that's what increases your ability to produce value.

In his book *The Seven Habits of Highly Effective People*, Stephen Covey calls this production versus production capability. Let's say you personally are able to produce $20,000 a year. If you spent $10,000 of that on yourself becoming better at producing well, that $20,000 a year could quickly become $50,000 a year. And if you then spend $20,000 on yourself, that $50,000 could become $100,00 or $150,000 or $200,000. So investing in yourself — in your clarity, in your purpose, in your ability to execute — is probably the straightest line to increasing that production capability.

Obviously, there's also the traditional sense of investing, in which you take your extra money and invest it into real estate, stocks and bonds and so on. Now, if I do a proper job investing in real estate, I could see between a 15 to 25% return year over year. But by properly investing in myself as an entrepreneur, I can see a 50 to 100% return year over year. I actually had Jim Dew, of Dew Wealth Management, come on my podcast and talk about that. And he said that they tell their clients to diversify and invest in multiple products, but first to make sure they're investing in themselves. Invest in your entrepreneurial business, because that will have the greatest return for you.

And it's not just the business that deserves investment. Remember the Five Spokes? Each one of them will benefit from investment. Some people might consider going on a date night with their spouse an expense: I would consider it an investment in my relationship with Maddy. Some people would consider a cold plunge an expense; I consider it an investment in my health.

Money Stories

Most people have at least a few beliefs around money that they would be well-served to change. Remember: your beliefs are not necessarily true, and it's your responsibility to decide if you want to keep an old belief or change it.

Most of us are literally given a relationship with money, from a young age, whether it's from our parents, our religion, our community, the media we consume, or all of the above. Your money stories are formed very young, often by people who are not thinking about what they're teaching you. Some families view money as pure evil and the kids absorb that. Some kids will grow up hating money because it takes their parents away from them and back to work all the time. Others learn that "money doesn't grow on trees" and that scarcity is just waiting to get you. We develop these stories young and we hold onto them without revisiting whether they're true or if they're still serving us.

For those of us who grew up in disadvantaged families, we can end up with a money mindset that drives us to be very frugal, to save and to be very risk-averse with money. It can also create an unhealthy desire for money — that money is the source of happiness and peace. We work with a lot of entrepreneurs that come from very poor and humble upbringings, and many of them start with an unhealthy attachment to making money and being successful. And eventually we actually have to break that attachment down the line, because it's coming from a place of fear, instead of a place of purpose. We need to help them start feeling secure and at peace independent of what their bank account says right now.

For those who grew up in wealthy families, there's a whole other set of problems. You might believe that money is the most important thing in life and it's worth sacrificing everything else to get more. Or on the other hand, you might have seen your parents working far too much, and you might internalize that money destroys families. When we work with entrepreneurs from these backgrounds, it's much more about helping them to see money as a tool, that's not intrinsically good or bad, but that it's within their power to control and that they can choose how they want to behave with their wealth. In the end it's not their fault that they grow up with money, so they shouldn't feel guilty about it. It just means they need to use that money wisely to help the world: "To whom much is given, much will be required," as it says in the Bible.

Now, just because you grew up rich or grew up poor doesn't mean you're definitely going to have these specific beliefs. There are so many variables that go into our money stories, and it's up to you to spend some time figuring out the lessons you absorbed early in your life, what you believe now, and what you want to believe in the future.

Reframing Your College Debt

A lot of people feel slighted by their college experience, and if that's where you are right now, that's okay. You invested all this money, you spent years studying, you worked your ass off, and now you're stuck doing something that's unfulfilling and is not paying down your debt like you want it to.

I get it. That is a shitty place to be, and I know because I was there a few years ago. I went to UCLA. I worked my ass off for five years — rent in the area was more than my college tuition, and I came out the other side of my degree with $120,000 worth of debt. Now, I got a good job. A really good job. I was able to pay off my debt relatively quickly, compared to most people that I know. But I was still terrified about investing in myself because I had been burned so badly: $120,000 to spend my time doing something that sucked? Why would I pay more to risk more of the same? That's the way the human brain works, right? "I paid this money, I put in all this work, and I got a shitty outcome. So if I pay more money, put in more work, why would I believe I'd get a different outcome?"

Look: it's not your fault if you think that way about investing in yourself. That is the way that society has programmed us to think for many years, but now you're conscious enough to know that it's not true. That's the first step. College was a $120,000 lesson for me, but I also did get a ton of value out of it. I got friends that are going to be lifelong friends. I got an experience that I probably would never change for the world. So even though it didn't produce the outcome that I wanted, did I get value out of it? Absolutely. Can I go back and look at the lessons and figure out what they can bring me in the future? Yes. But if you never reflect on it, and learn the lesson from your past experiences, then you can never grow into the future. We have to accept that college may have not gotten us where we wanted to go, but that's a problem with college — not a problem with investing in yourself.

When I first quit Cisco, I spent nearly $40,000 on different programs, masterminds, and coaches. Sometimes a coaching client will ask which one was the best investment (because obviously, we all just want to go straight for the proven choice). Honestly, the best investment I made when I first started my coaching business was a $12,000 mastermind that taught me literally nothing. If I were to go back and do it all over, that's the one that's the most important to me, for two reasons.

One: I learned who I didn't want to be as a coach and what I didn't want to do. Sometimes learning what you don't want to do is just as important as what you do want. Two: it gave me the opportunity to face my fear and keep investing. I put that $12,000 investment on a credit card. It was the first time I went into debt investing in myself and I got literally nothing from it — it was all outdated principles from a decade ago. It had minimal support and coaching.

But the next couple of programs and mentors I invested in completed the 'combination lock' for me and the door to my future swung open. Had I never been given the opportunity to face my fear and invest again, I would not have had those next opportunities and I would not be the same person I am today. So whatever you believe in — whether it's God or Mother Earth or the universe, I want you to ask for courage. Ask for the opportunity to be courageous to keep investing in yourself. You will be given the opportunity, but you are the one that has to step through the door.

SIXTEEN
RELATIONSHIP MASTERY

"Truth is, I'll never know all there is to know about you just as you will never know all there is to know about me. Humans are by nature too complicated to be understood fully. So, we can choose either to approach our fellow human beings with suspicion or to approach them with an open mind, a dash of optimism and a great deal of candor."

TOM HANKS

In the end, the only things that bring you joy are human connection, growth, and accomplishing things you care about. Your relationships will help you with all three of those, and so you need to treat your relationships just like you treat everything else. Whether it's your romantic relationship, your family relationships, your friendships or your business relationships, they all need care, focused attention and ownership to thrive —

the same principles that we've talked about all through this book also apply here.

In any relationship, you need to take 100% ownership. Not 50%, hoping the other person will make up the difference. Because if you and the other person each take 50%, then whose fault is it when something goes wrong? Well, it's *their* 50%, obviously! But if you take 100% ownership for a relationship, you can never put any blame on the other person. Take full ownership, acknowledge it when you're not good enough, and do the work to become good enough. This is how Maddy and I treat our relationship: yes, we're both already phenomenal people, if I do say so myself, but do we still have room to grow in our relationship? Absolutely. The moment one of us thinks we're perfect, or that the other person is the one with the problem, that's the moment a relationship starts to crumble.

Of course, to create that kind of communication with anyone else, you have to be radically honest with yourself. Most people are afraid to be honest with themselves. It's uncomfortable and it forces you to change, which no one likes. But if you can't be honest with yourself, how can you ever be honest with somebody else? You have to be able to acknowledge the things you're afraid of, the things that you want, what drives you, what makes you feel loved. What we all want is to have relationships with other people who understand all those things about us, but if we can't express them to ourselves first, you'll never be able to express it to someone else.

Remember we talked about the seven environments? One of those environments is your thoughts, the way that you think — that is your relationship with yourself. That is something you need to take full ownership of. It's critical to understand that you're probably not where you need to be just yet, and to have faith that you can get there. All the work about setting goals and getting clarity around how you want to be as a person and who you want to be as a person — all of that is building radical candor into your relationship with yourself, so that you can reach out and really connect with others.

Radical Candor

Being extremely honest is hard. Being friends or spouses with someone who is extremely honest can be even harder. Because sometimes the truth hurts.

But in the end, open and honest communication (to the point that it's scary) is the only way to build a deeply strong relationship. This is what we call Radical Candor.

Radical candor is about taking ownership for properly communicating in each of your relationships, so that the other person knows how you're feeling, what you need and how to make sure this relationship continues in a positive and healthy way. So many times we assume that somebody else just knows what we're thinking, but the vast majority of the time, they don't. They can't. If you want your relationships to thrive, you have to cultivate a desire to be so open and honest with your communication, that there is no room for either of you to be left wondering what the other person is thinking or feeling. Once you know specifically what somebody wants and needs, it becomes very easy to keep the relationship working. But if there are hidden agendas (usually caused by fear — fear of scaring someone away, fear of not being understood), that's how things start to fall apart. No two people ever think exactly the same thing. You will never have the same exact view on things as the other person, and if you're not learning how to communicate so that you actually understand each other, it's very difficult to work things out.

When Maddy and I first met, we talked about things within

the first 48 hours that I had never talked about with the people closest to me, let alone a girl I just met.

- Our biggest fears and insecurities in life
- Sexual preferences and polyamory
- Where we would live if we got married
- How many kids we each wanted and by what age
- What we liked about each other and what we would change

Yeah... crazy opening convos.

But that openness and honesty was necessary. We lived 9000 miles apart at the time so we needed to understand all the details to figure out if there was something possible between us, and we needed that understanding fast.

In this book we've talked a lot about clarity. As you develop more clarity in your own thinking and emotions, you will also need to start communicating that clarity, without holding anything back out of those fears we just mentioned. When you start to discover new information about yourself, it's key to be clear with the other person about what is changing. Maddy and I are practicing this all the time. When both people, in any kind of relationship, are continuing to grow and move, you can either get closer together or further apart, and the difference is communication. If either of you are not communicating the change that's going on inside you, you will start to diverge from each other — often until it's too late. That's why Maddy and I have weekly and monthly check-ins about what we're thinking about and how we're feeling about our lives. The communication channels are constantly open.

For example, when Maddy first moved here to the US, it was an exciting adventure. But over time, she started missing certain things about Australia and other places we've been, so we started talking about our options. Do we move to Australia for a while? Would Costa Rica do it? Now, having these conversations doesn't mean that we're just going to uproot everything when one of us isn't feeling great. It just means we're feeling out what would be ideal for both of us, where we can work together to make sure we're both continuing to thrive, individually and together.

We don't judge each other during these conversations, we're not jumping to conclusions about why things have changed — it's a constant exploration that requires total honesty and openness to work. We have these conversations constantly, because something is always changing, we're always growing and evolving. And there's no denying it can be uncomfortable sometimes. The thought of moving to Australia challenges me a lot, because my business is so rooted in the US. But it would also present me with a huge opportunity for personal growth. Maddy knows that, and it would be understandable for her to be scared of raising that possibility with me. But if she didn't do it, or if I shut down the conversation out of hand because that possibility is inconvenient for me, we would risk drifting apart. Over years of not raising what we want, or refusing to talk about other possibilities, maybe we would drift so far apart that we wouldn't be able to bridge the chasm anymore. That's not acceptable to either of us.

Often the conversation will ultimately come down to asking yourself, *Am I willing to do XYZ for this relationship?* Sometimes the answer might be no, and then the question becomes, *Am I saying no from a place of fear or a place of purpose?* When you honestly answer those questions internally, you can have a powerful conversation with the other person, so that both of you can continue moving in the direction that's right for you.

It's totally okay if you discover, from that place of purpose, that you are no longer moving in the same direction. Every relationship ebbs and flows. Let me give you an example from my business: the first person I ever hired full-time was an awesome guy (who is now a close friend) named Joshua Church. He was with me for the first few years of my business. He believed in the idea before it was even starting to work. He had so much faith in it, and he was there with me figuring shit out, breaking stuff, fixing it — and I thought he was gonna be with me forever. One day he called me up and said he'd had an offer to go work in a startup with Robert Downey Jr... and I knew immediately that I had to just be happy for him. I'm a good boss, but I'm not Iron Man! So I told him I was happy for him, gave him everything he needed to go do this next thing , and told him that he would always have a home at High Impact Coaching if he wanted it — all he had to do was ask and he'd be back on board.

He went away for the next few months, and got some amazing experience in his new roles, but eventually felt like he was doing it for the wrong reasons. He called me back up and asked if we could make some adjustments at HIC so that he could make it his home again. Of course I said yes. I loved working with him and he deserved whatever he needed to make it work. Two years later, he's still on as our director of operations. He's such a huge asset to our team, and even more now after he had room to experiment and try something else. But if we did not have a foundation of radical candor, none of that would have been possible. I would have been surprised and hurt by his decision to leave. He might not have told me the truth about why he wanted to leave, and then I might not have welcomed him back. But we did have that foundation, and so I totally got why that gig appealed to him, and understood that it wasn't about me or my business.

People are adjusting and changing all the time, and we're

changing with them. But the only way that we can do that is through radical candor. We have these conversations on a very regular basis — every three months we check in with every employee, because life moves quickly and what people want and need and dream about changes quickly too.

Have Faith

I decided a long time ago that I was going to have faith in my relationships — to just trust that in the end, it'll all be good. So many people do crazy things in their relationships, because they're afraid that something bad is going to happen in the relationship.

From a business standpoint, if I'm afraid a team member might leave, I might not give them the opportunities they deserve, I might not give them the raises or the promotions they really deserve. That's ass-backwards: if I had faith that this person is going to give their all, and that person is going to do their best, I'm going to treat them with the respect they deserve give them more opportunities — and because I'm treating them well, they're going to stick around for longer.

Same thing in romantic relationships. I have faith that Maddy and I are going to be together forever. There's no question for me there. I don't get jealous when I see another guy looking at her, I don't get jealous when she wants to go do something without me, I don't feel less worthy if she wants to go spend time with friends or family rather than do something with me, because I have faith that we're going the right direction together to where we both really want to be. I'm not afraid of losing her, because I have faith in our relationship.

Remember that one way or another, just like life, all relationships come to an end. It might be a break-up, a death, a relocation, and just as we talked about the need to accept the reality of dying, we also need to accept the reality of the end of each relationship. When you start to really accept that this will happen, the fear starts to go away: the fear of losing a friend, the fear of losing a loved one, the fear of losing a business partner. It will always be hard. It's okay to grieve the end of a relationship. But every relationship will be in your life for a season — maybe short, maybe long — but everybody's moving. Everybody's doing their own thing. And if you accept that all relationships come to an end, then you start to really embrace the joy and connection you have during the time you do have together. Whether it's for a 70-year marriage, or it's someone you had one conversation with at a coffee shop, you will really appreciate that time, because you know you won't have it forever.

Find The Gratitude

Everything happens for you, not to you. When you're in a relationship, you're gonna have both positive and negative experiences — that's just reality. If you focus on the negative, you'll view the relationship as more negative. If you focus on the positive, you'll view the relationship as more positive. This is something that Maddy is incredibly good at. I will be the first to admit that I do a lot of shit she would probably rather I didn't. But she focuses on all the things I do that she can be grateful and appreciative for. Every night before we go to bed, we tell each other two things: one thing we're grateful for, and one thing that we love about the other person. Those are the last two things that we think about before we go to sleep.

If you think about the dynamics of relationships where you focus on what you're grateful for compared to focusing on what you don't like, you'll see that the behaviors are completely different. When we get praised for good things, we want to do more of those good things, and the negative things tend to start fading away. But if we get nagged or criticised, we don't want to do anything at all. Our dog Aspen has made me realize that I'm basically a sheep dog: if I get praised for doing something, I'm going to do it again. So when Maddy expresses gratitude that I helped do the laundry, or that I took out the trash before she asked, that's like my little reward. Instead of a bit of dried liver like we give Aspen, I get a bit of gratitude. Of course I'm going to take the trash cans out again. Of course I'm going to do the dishes and help with the laundry, because she's so grateful that I help out with it. Do I enjoy taking the bins out? No, nobody enjoys that. Do I love doing laundry? No, so boring, but doing stuff like this is a chance to help each other find gratitude.

Apart from your relationship with yourself, your relationships with others are the most important part of your life. Whether it's your spouse, your family, your friends or your colleagues, the people you spend your time with will have a huge influence on you and will significantly influence your sense of meaning, joy and fulfilment. So go all in on them. Don't hold back from people. Be radically honest, be vulnerable, show up. Do the things that are hard and uncomfortable simply because they will make your relationships better. Keep your relationships firmly in the front of your mind and cultivate them as carefully as you do any other part of your life.

CONCLUSION

True success in life is about mastery. Everything we've talked about in this book is easy to understand once you see it all laid out: how to learn, how to reason, how to think critically, how to find clarity, how to set yourself up for success, how to implement, how to review and improve — all that you can understand in a moment. But it will take you years to master this. It will take time, it'll take repetition, it'll take intentional, incremental improvements. There's no short-term, microwave solution to creating the life you really want. It's not about knowledge. You can easily get knowledge any time you actually need it — the more difficult thing is to apply the knowledge you now already have so that you achieve mastery and wisdom.

In this book you've learned everything you need to start moving towards that mastery. If you can stick with these concepts, practice them over and over until they are second nature, you will inevitably move towards that life you've dreamt of, a life where you have all the money, meaning and freedom you want to achieve great things with the time you have here on this earth. Now the real work begins.

Printed in Great Britain
by Amazon